# MAN ON A MISSION

# MAN ON A
# MISSION

## JAMES MEREDITH
## AND THE BATTLE
## OF OLE MISS

Written by
**ARAM
GOUDSOUZIAN**

Illustrated by
**BILL MURRAY**

Edited by
**VIJAY SHAH**

The University of Arkansas Press
Fayetteville ■ 2022

ISBN: 978-1-68226-212-2
eISBN: 978-1-61075-779-9

26  25  24  23  22    5  4  3  2  1

Manufactured in the United States of America

∞ The paper used in this publication meets the minimum requirements of the American National Standard for Permanence of Paper for Printed Library Materials Z39.48-1984.

Cataloging-in-Publication Data on file at the Library of Congress

Dedicated to James Meredith, his family,
and all who bravely strive for justice

# CONTENTS

# PREFACE

James Meredith loves Mississippi. At the same time, he wants to destroy its racial system based on white supremacy. He also believes deeply in the power of education. For these reasons, Meredith applied to the University of Mississippi (a.k.a. Ole Miss) and provoked a legal drama to gain admission. The ensuing Battle of Ole Miss changed American history. Meredith showed enormous courage during the 1962–63 academic year, when he faced constant threats and harassment. He deserves the regard of every American.

We created this book to bring the story of James Meredith to a larger and younger audience. We hope that it will be used in classrooms, placed on bookshelves at home, and checked out of libraries. We appreciate the support of Mr. Meredith, who has championed our project from the beginning.

Portraying Meredith poses quite a challenge. He is fiercely individualistic. At times, he can be unyielding. He wants radical change, but he holds conservative ideas about how to achieve success in life. These are the same characteristics, however, that made him such an important figure in American history.

*Man on a Mission* is inspired by Meredith's memoir, *Three Years in Mississippi*, which was originally published in 1966. As a result, this book often uses the language of his memoir. In some speech bubbles, we include the word "Negro," which was a common and accepted term at that time. Yet when depicting the racial slurs that white segregationists hurled at Meredith, we chose to use "n****r." We wanted to convey the nasty hatred that he endured but avoid spelling out that poisonous term.

We illustrate Meredith's dramatic account with a blend of historical substance and artistic creativity. Some panels modify old photographs with innovative flourishes, while others rely on hand-drawn pictures, based on our historically informed imagination. As we depict Meredith throughout his long and eventful life, he appears in many different forms.

After the graphic story, you will find a set of questions to help you think about James Meredith's life and mission. We have also provided a short essay that describes the research for this book and the wider history that shaped it. Finally, we have included a bibliography that lists some major works on James Meredith, the Ole Miss crisis, and civil rights in Mississippi.

We are grateful for the encouragement of the Meredith family. We extend thanks to the artist Suzi Altman, who enabled us to use her photograph of Mr. Meredith and children as a model for one panel. Further, we hold deep appreciation for David Scott Cunningham, Janet Foxman, Liz Lester, and the entire staff at the University of Arkansas Press.

We hope that *Man on a Mission* is unique and compelling, with an important story to tell—just like James Meredith himself.

# INTRODUCTION

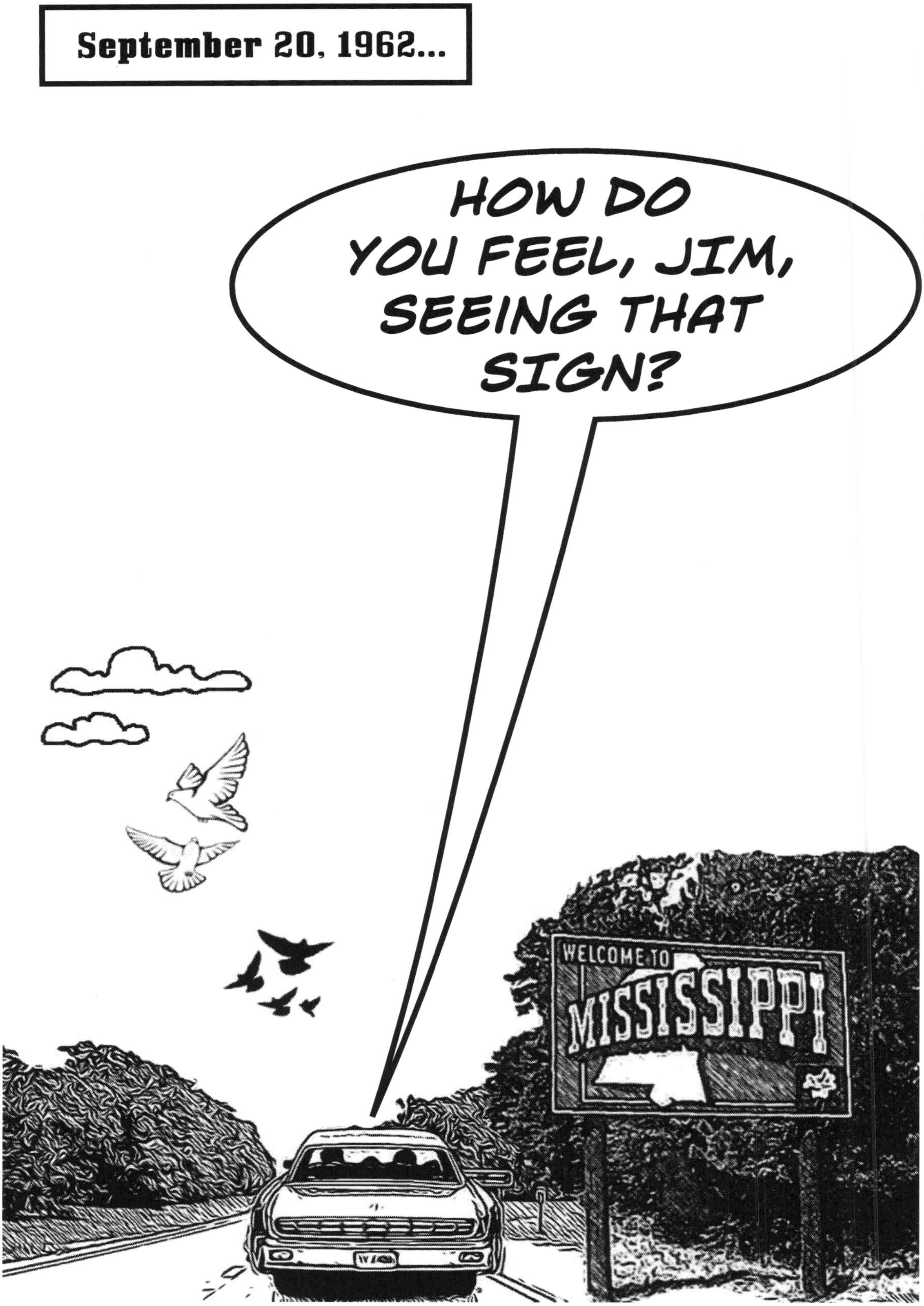
September 20, 1962...
HOW DO YOU FEEL, JIM, SEEING THAT SIGN?
WELCOME TO
MISSISSIPPI

JOY, FOR THE ONLY LAND IN WHICH I FEEL AT HOME.

SADNESS, BECAUSE IN A RICH LAND OF PLENTY, MY PEOPLE STILL SUFFER.

I'LL GET MY SHARE OF LAND OR DIE TRYING!

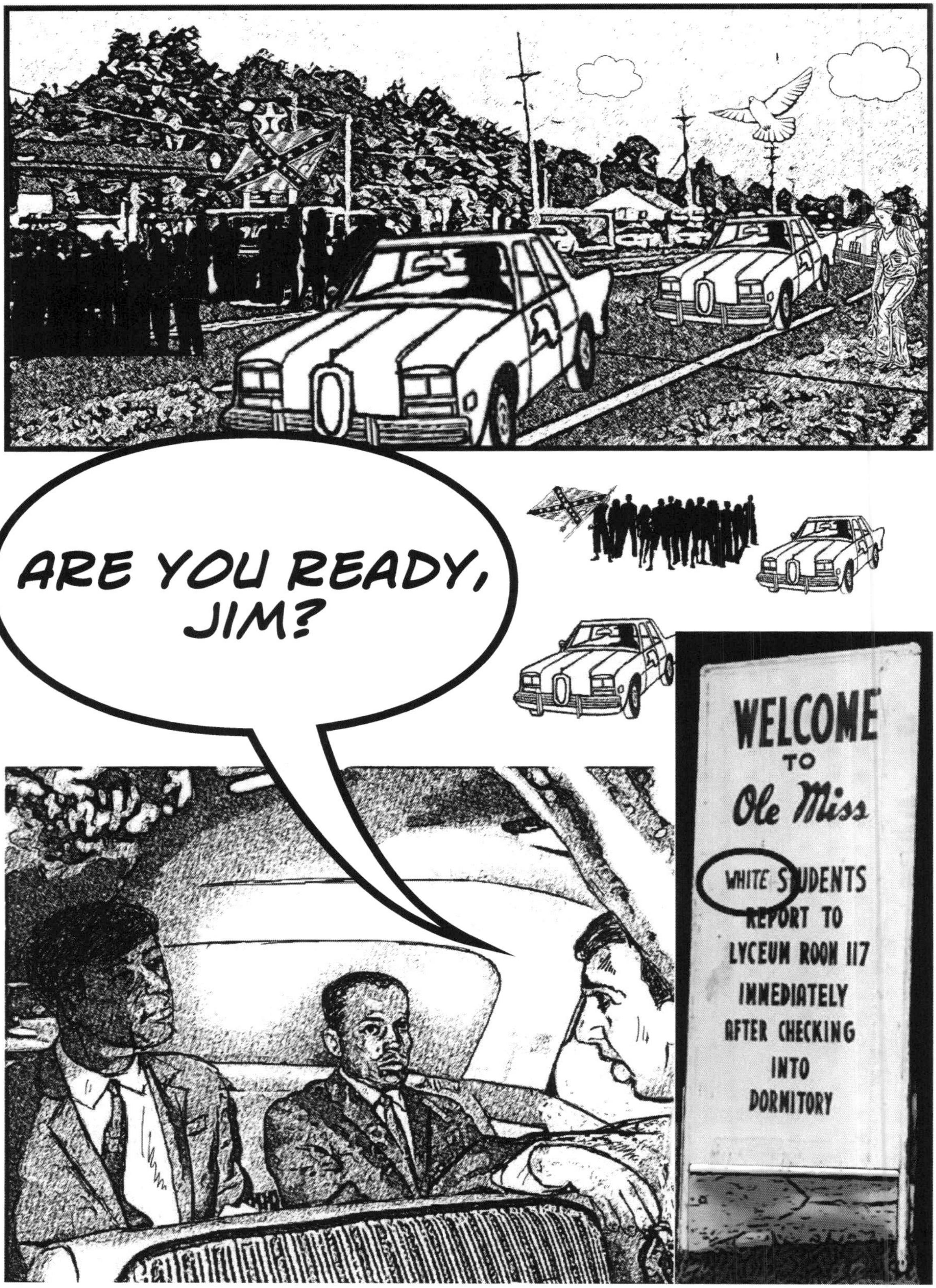
ARE YOU READY, JIM?
WELCOME TO Ole Miss
WHITE STUDENTS REPORT TO LYCEUM ROOM 117 IMMEDIATELY AFTER CHECKING INTO DORMITORY

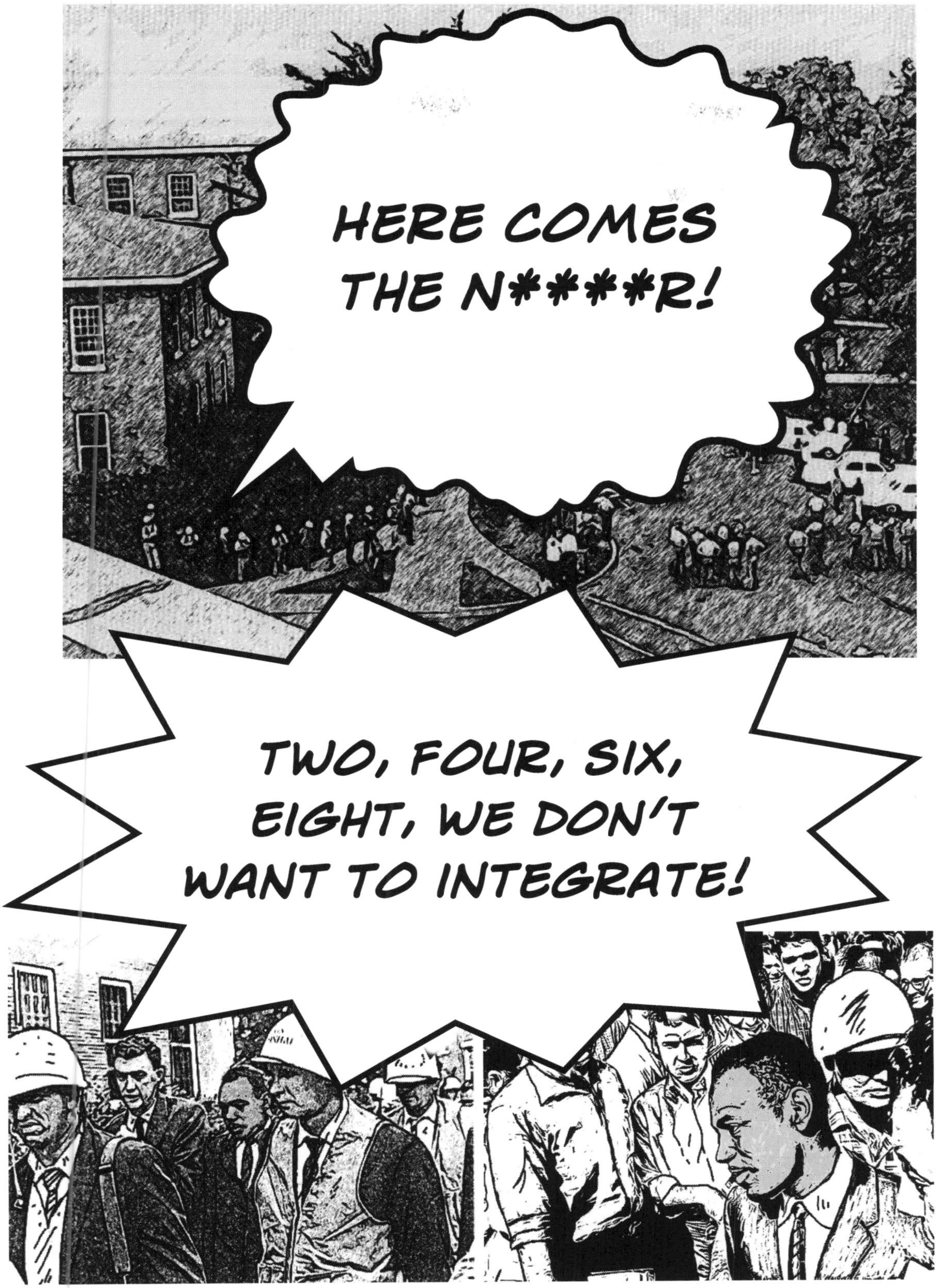
HERE COMES THE N****R!
TWO, FOUR, SIX, EIGHT, WE DON'T WANT TO INTEGRATE!

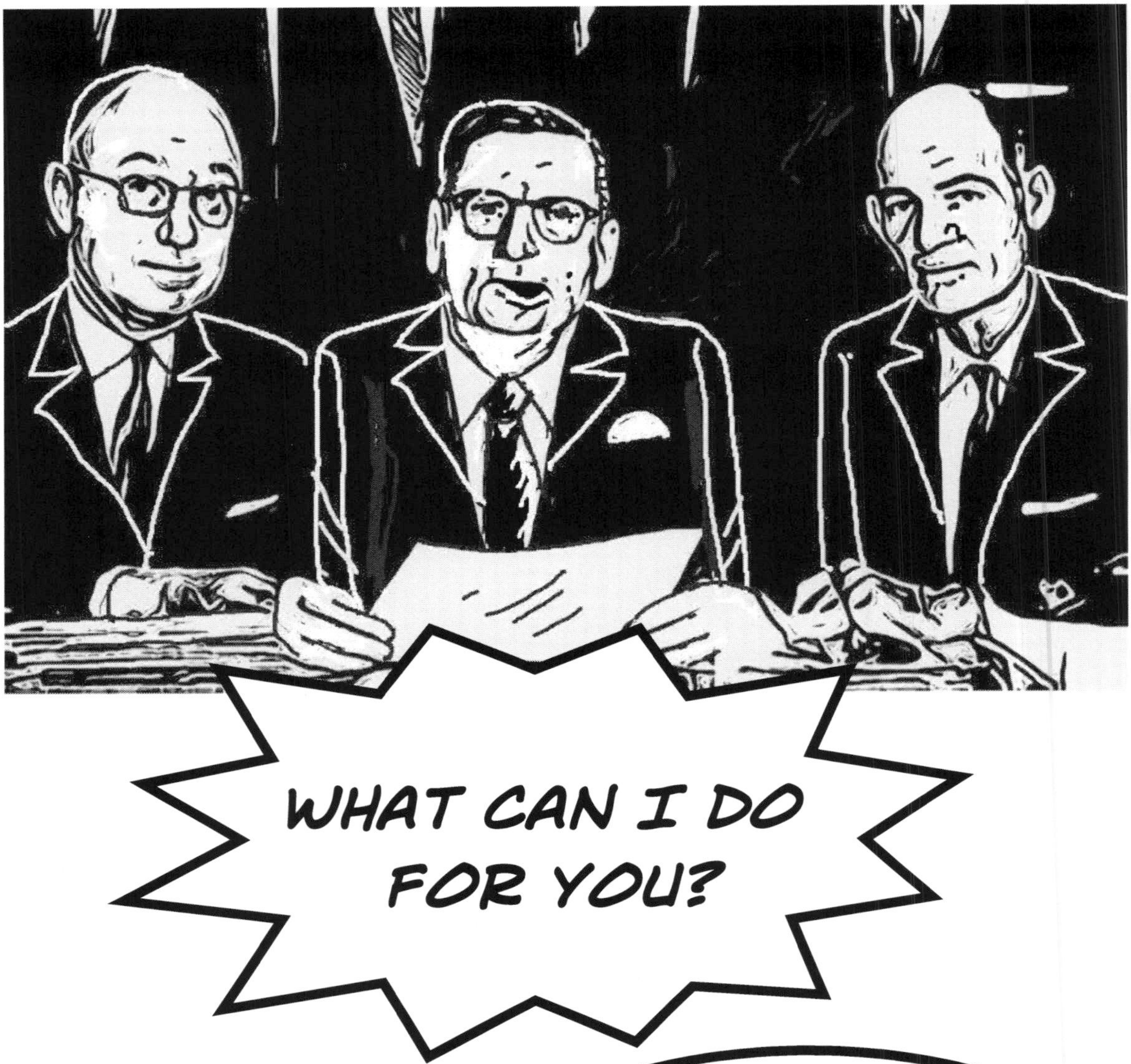
WHAT CAN I DO FOR YOU?

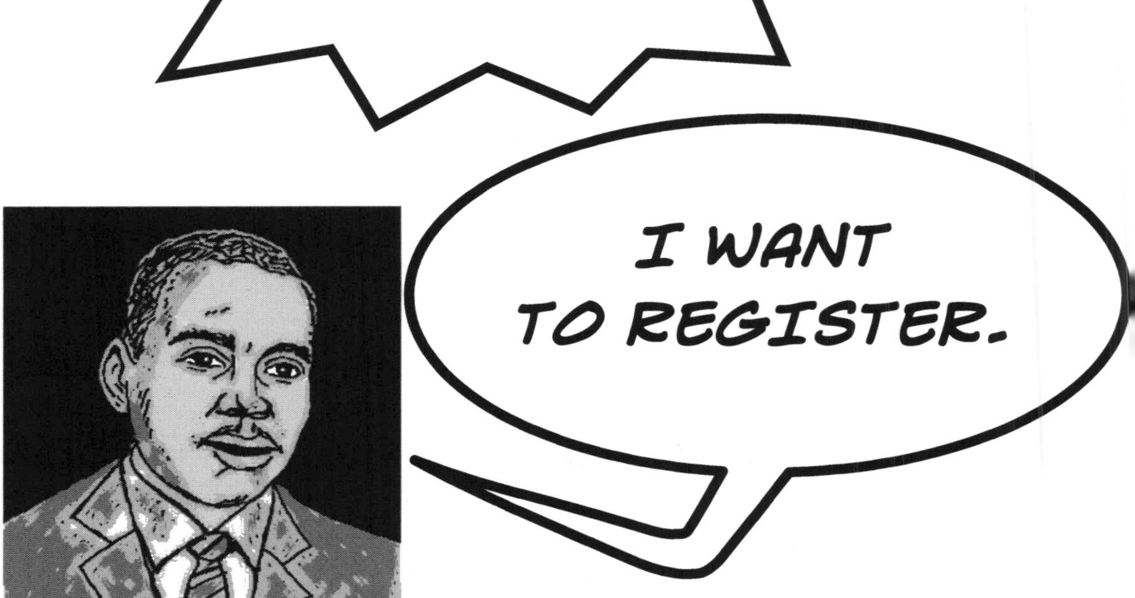
I WANT TO REGISTER.

# I, ROSS R. BARNETT, GOVERNOR OF THE STATE OF MISSISSIPPI, HEREBY REFUSE ADMISSION TO JAMES H. MEREDITH AS A STUDENT TO THE UNIVERSITY OF MISSISSIPPI.

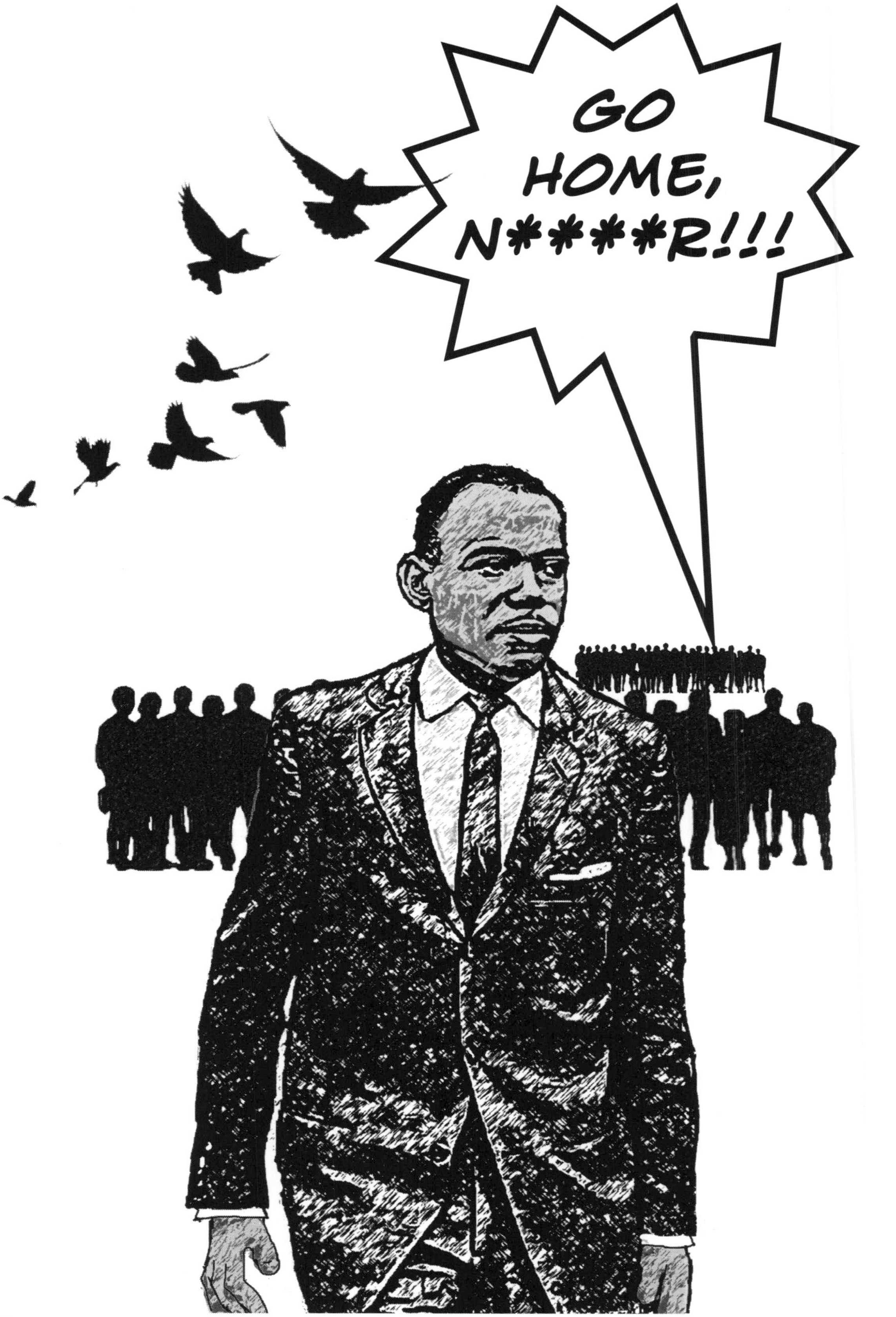
GO HOME, N****R!!!

THIS WAS MY FIRST ATTEMPT TO REGISTER AS A STUDENT AT THE UNIVERSITY OF MISSISSIPPI, ALSO KNOWN AS OLE MISS.

THE GOVERNOR HIMSELF TURNED ME AWAY, BECAUSE OLE MISS WAS SEGREGATED, A SYMBOL OF WHITE POWER.

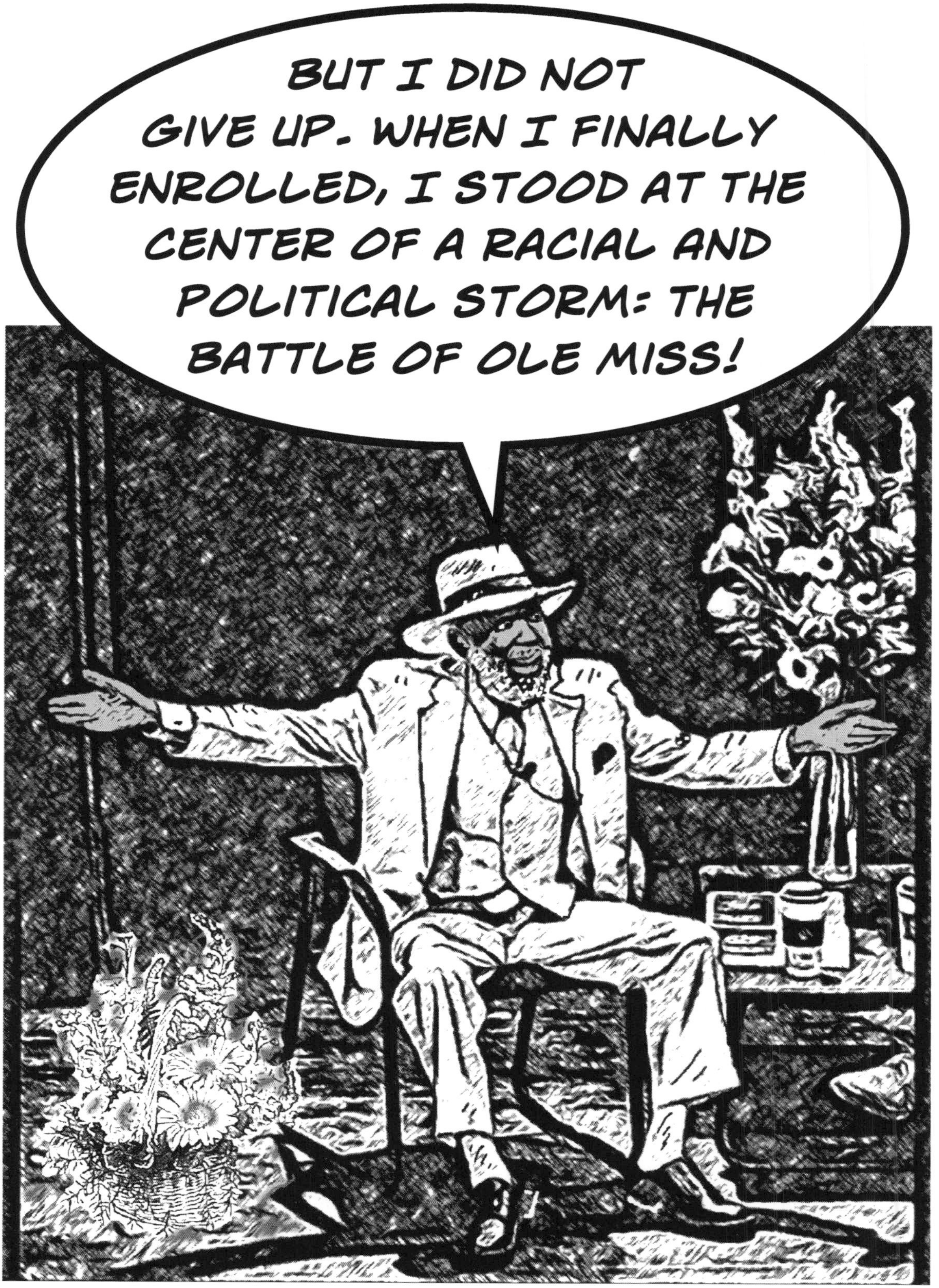
BUT I DID NOT GIVE UP. WHEN I FINALLY ENROLLED, I STOOD AT THE CENTER OF A RACIAL AND POLITICAL STORM: THE BATTLE OF OLE MISS!

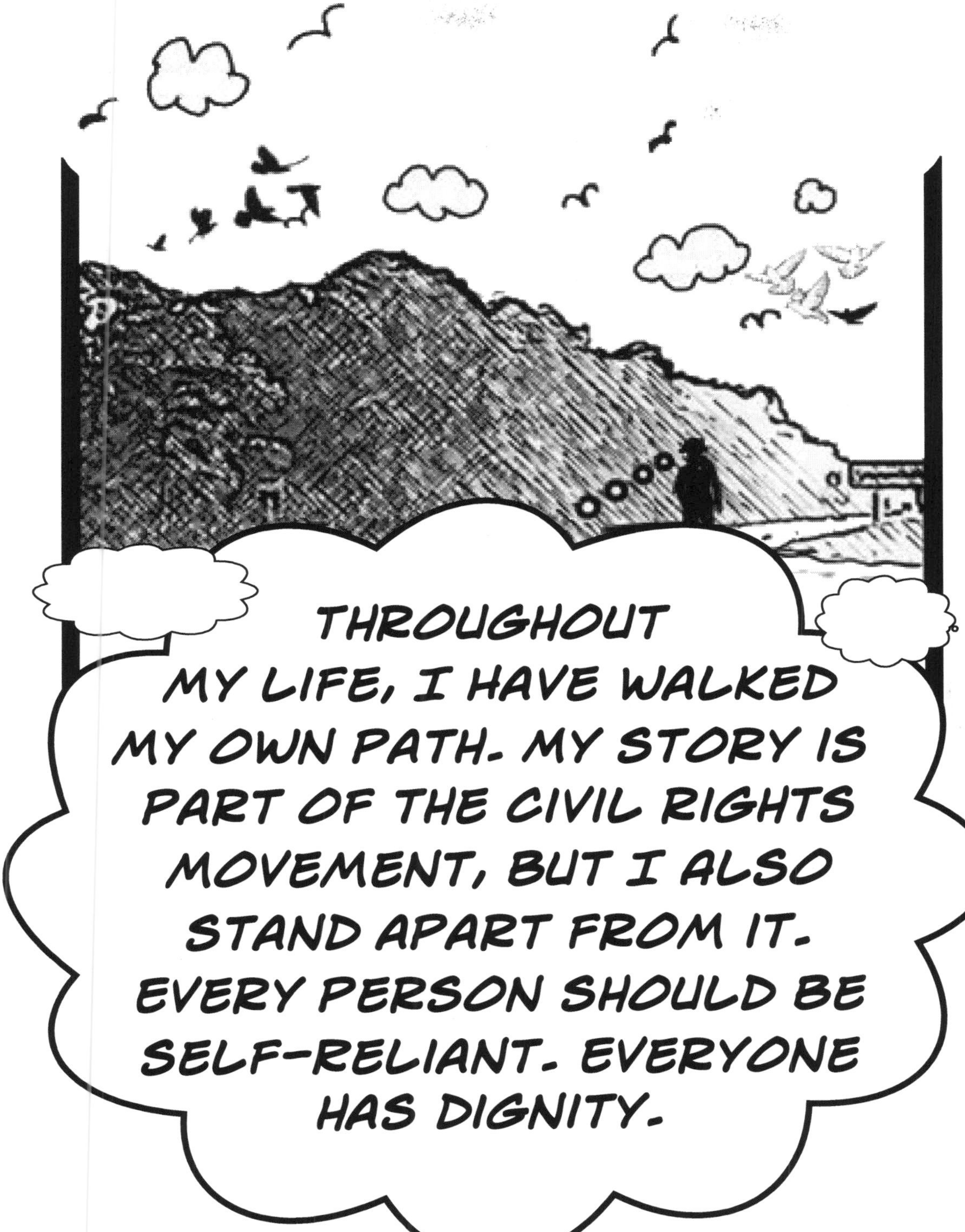
THROUGHOUT MY LIFE, I HAVE WALKED MY OWN PATH. MY STORY IS PART OF THE CIVIL RIGHTS MOVEMENT, BUT I ALSO STAND APART FROM IT. EVERY PERSON SHOULD BE SELF-RELIANT. EVERYONE HAS DIGNITY.

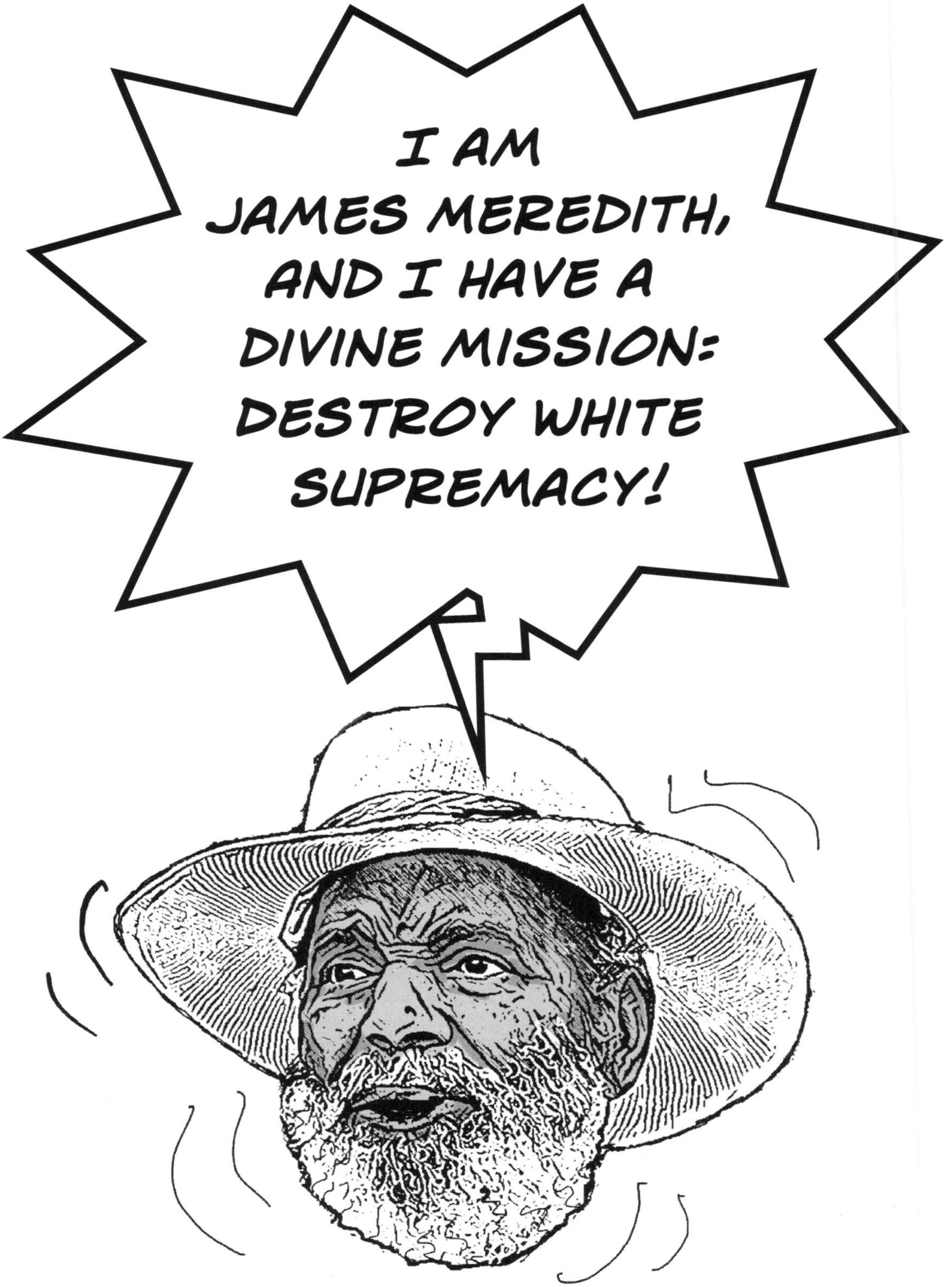
I AM JAMES MEREDITH, AND I HAVE A DIVINE MISSION: DESTROY WHITE SUPREMACY!

# CHAPTER ONE:

# MISSISSIPPI AND ME

ON OUR 84-ACRE FARM IN KOSCIUSKO, MISSISSIPPI, MY FATHER TAUGHT ME THE TRUE MEANING OF LIFE: DEATH IS PREFERABLE TO INDIGNITY!

WE ARE THE CHOSEN FAMILY. IT IS YOUR DUTY AND RESPONSIBILITY TO LEAD OUR PEOPLE TO THEIR PLACE IN THIS WORLD.

OUR HOME HAD NO RUNNING
WATER, AND THE WIND BLEW
THROUGH CRACKS IN THE WALLS.
BUT THERE WAS PRIDE AND ORDER.

OUR LAND WAS THE KEY
TO OUR INDEPENDENCE. WE NEVER
WORKED FOR WHITE FOLKS.

15

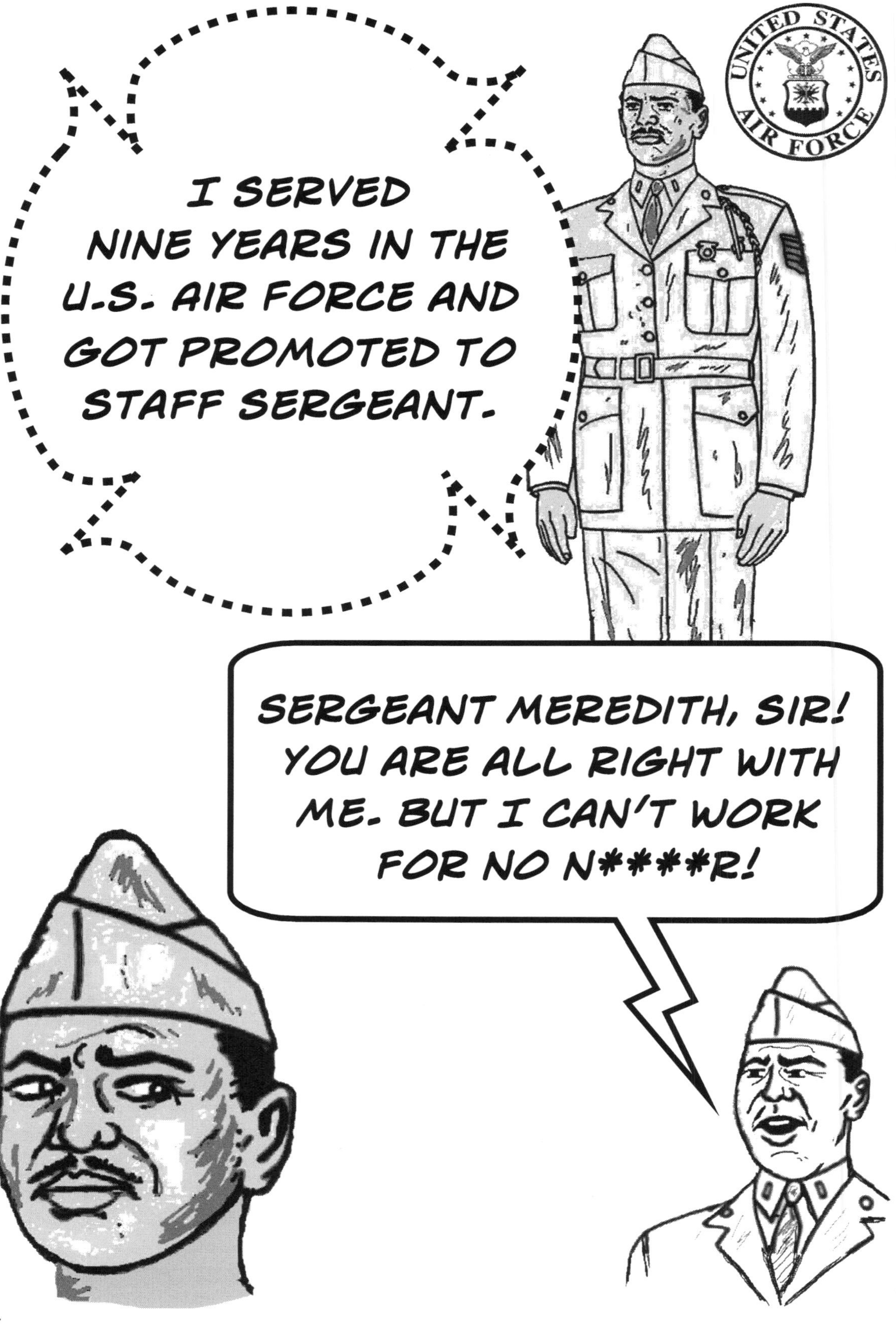
UNITED STATES AIR FORCE
I SERVED NINE YEARS IN THE U.S. AIR FORCE AND GOT PROMOTED TO STAFF SERGEANT.
SERGEANT MEREDITH, SIR! YOU ARE ALL RIGHT WITH ME. BUT I CAN'T WORK FOR NO N****R!

THE AIR FORCE BASE IN JAPAN WAS THE ONLY PLACE WHERE I HAVE NOT FELT THE AIR OF DIFFERENCE AT BEING BLACK. BUT WHEN I THOUGHT ABOUT THE STAIN AND DISGRACE WHITE SUPREMACY CAST ON MY COUNTRY, I GOT SICK TO MY STOMACH. I HAD TO RETURN TO MISSISSIPPI!

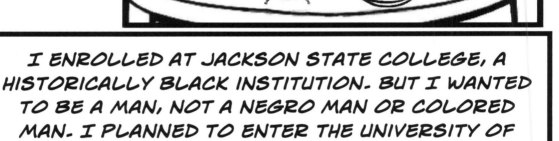

**JANUARY 21, 1961**

**REGISTRAR
UNIVERSITY OF
MISSISSIPPI**

**DEAR SIR,
PLEASE SEND ME AN APPLICATION
TO YOUR SCHOOL.**

I ENROLLED AT JACKSON STATE COLLEGE, A HISTORICALLY BLACK INSTITUTION. BUT I WANTED TO BE A MAN, NOT A NEGRO MAN OR COLORED MAN. I PLANNED TO ENTER THE UNIVERSITY OF MISSISSIPPI FOR THE GOOD OF MY PEOPLE, MY COUNTRY, MY STATE, MY FAMILY, AND MYSELF.

AFTER THE 1954 SUPREME COURT DECISION IN "BROWN V. BOARD OF EDUCATION," PUBLIC EDUCATION SERVED AS A BATTLEGROUND FOR RACIAL EQUALITY. MANY AMERICANS WERE INSPIRED BY THE LITTLE ROCK NINE IN ARKANSAS.

BUT THE "BROWN" DECISION ALSO INTENSIFIED WHITE RESISTANCE. THE SEGREGATIONIST CITIZENS' COUNCIL STARTED IN MISSISSIPPI. POWERFUL WHITES SUCH AS SENATOR JAMES EASTLAND BLOCKED THE INTEGRATION OF SCHOOLS.

MISSISSIPPI WAS NOTORIOUS FOR RACIST VIOLENCE. IN 1955, SOME WHITE MEN MURDERED EMMETT TILL, A 14-YEAR-OLD BOY VISITING FROM CHICAGO, BECAUSE HE MIGHT HAVE FLIRTED WITH A WHITE WOMAN.

AN ALL-WHITE JURY REFUSED TO FIND THE MURDERERS GUILTY.

WHITE AUTHORITIES CRUSHED EARLIER ATTEMPTS TO INTEGRATE HIGHER EDUCATION. IN 1958, CLENNON KING APPLIED TO THE UNIVERSITY OF MISSISSIPPI FOR A GRADUATE DEGREE IN HISTORY.

WHEN HE SHOWED UP TO REGISTER, THE POLICE CARRIED HIM AWAY, AND THE STATE COMMITTED HIM TO A PSYCHIATRIC HOSPITAL.

IN 1959, CLYDE KENNARD TRIED TO REGISTER AT MISSISSIPPI SOUTHERN COLLEGE. THE POLICE ARRESTED HIM ON TRUMPED-UP CHARGES OF SPEEDING AND ALCOHOL POSSESSION.

WHEN HE KEPT ON TRYING, THE STATE FRAMED HIM FOR STEALING CHICKEN FEED. HE SPENT MOST OF THE REST OF HIS LIFE IN BRUTAL PARCHMAN PRISON.

WHEN I FIRST APPLIED TO THE UNIVERSITY OF MISSISSIPPI, THE REGISTRAR TRIED TO DELAY, INSISTING THAT I MISSED DEADLINES AND LACKED PROPER MATERIALS.

AT THE SAME TIME, WHITES WERE HARASSING MY NEIGHBORS, TRYING TO SCARE ME.

YOU TELL THAT N****R TRYING TO GO TO OLE MISS THAT WE ARE GOING TO KILL HIM!

I WENT TO SEE MEDGAR EVERS, THE COURAGEOUS FIELD SECRETARY FOR THE MISSISSIPPI NAACP. HE INVESTIGATED CRIMES AGAINST BLACK PEOPLE FROM VOTER SUPPRESSION TO MURDER, WHILE LEADING BOYCOTTS AGAINST SEGREGATED PUBLIC FACILITIES.

YOU NEED A LAWYER. WRITE TO THURGOOD MARSHALL IN NEW YORK!

DESPITE MARSHALL'S MISGIVINGS, HE ASSIGNED THE CASE TO CONSTANCE BAKER MOTLEY.

THIS MAN HAS GOT TO BE CRAZY!

WHILE THE REGISTRAR'S OFFICE DELAYED AND DENIED MY APPLICATION, MRS. MOTLEY AND I CREATED A CAREFUL, DETAILED PAPER TRAIL TO SHOW THAT I WAS A LEGITIMATE APPLICANT.

BY 1961, THE CIVIL RIGHTS MOVEMENT WAS SHAKING UP MISSISSIPPI. THAT MARCH, NINE STUDENTS FROM TOUGALOO COLLEGE GOT ARRESTED AFTER DEMONSTRATING AT JACKSON PUBLIC LIBRARY.

I WATCHED THE ARRESTS OF THE FREEDOM RIDERS, WHO WERE INTEGRATING BUSES AND BUS STATIONS ACROSS THE SOUTH. HUNDREDS OF THEM ENDED UP IN PRISONS.

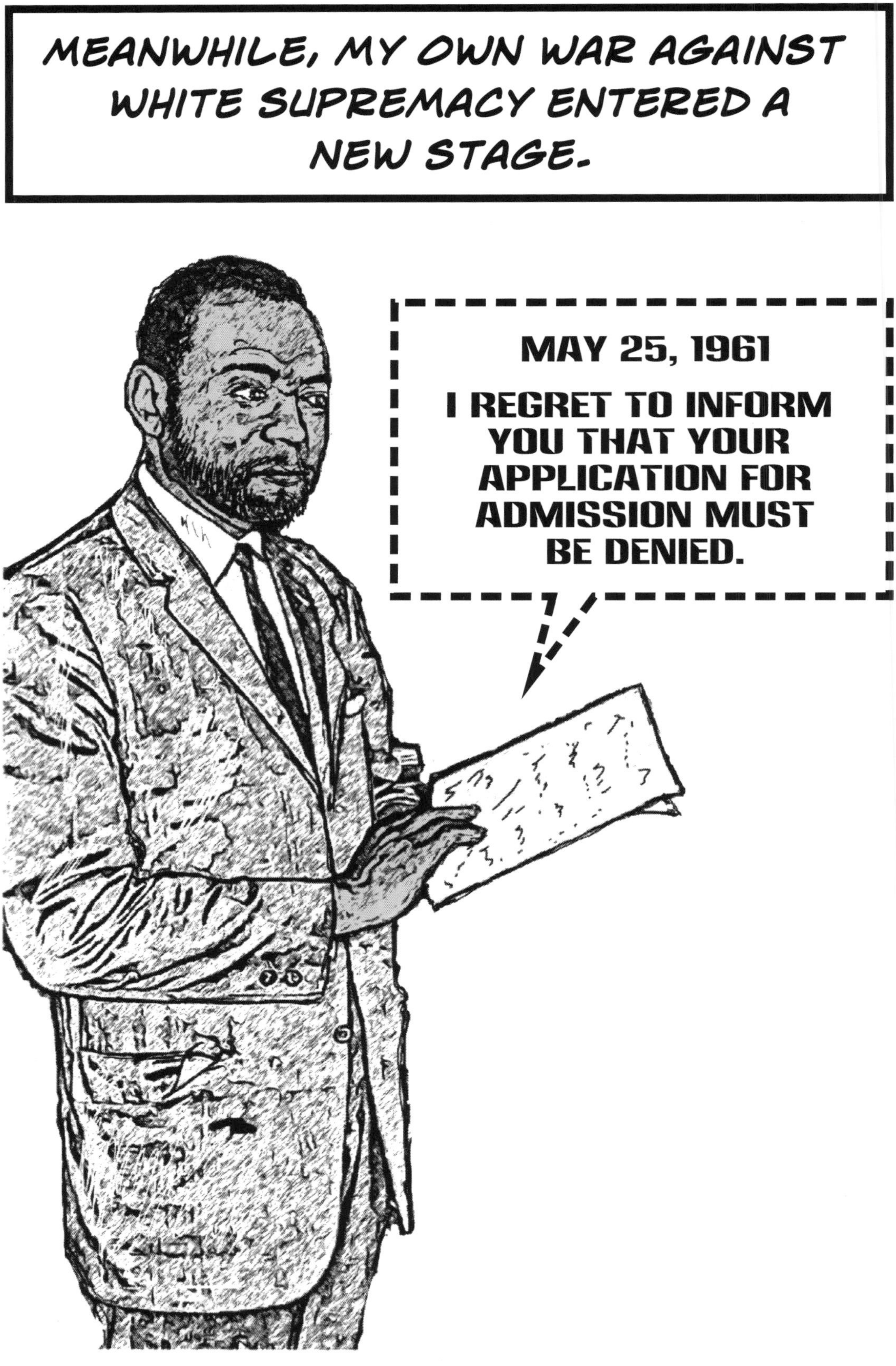
MEANWHILE, MY OWN WAR AGAINST WHITE SUPREMACY ENTERED A NEW STAGE.
MAY 25, 1961
I REGRET TO INFORM YOU THAT YOUR APPLICATION FOR ADMISSION MUST BE DENIED.

# CHAPTER TWO:
# THE LEGAL CHALLENGE

OUR TRIAL STARTED IN JUNE 1961.
AFTER SOME PRODDING FROM
MRS. MOTLEY TO PROJECT
A PROPER IMAGE,
I SHAVED MY BEARD.

THE STATE'S LAWYER, DUGAS SHANDS, WAS A MASTER AT WHAT I CALLED THE N****R TREATMENT. HE TRIED TO PROVOKE AND BREAK BLACK WITNESSES.

THE LAWYER'S TACTICS LED DOWN ROADS OF NO RETURN. WHITE FOLKS LIKE TO THINK THAT THEY KNOW BLACKS, BUT WE KNOW WHITES BETTER THAN THEY KNOW THEMSELVES.

I DREW STRENGTH AND INSPIRATION FROM MY COMMUNITY. EVERY COURT SESSION IN JACKSON WAS JAMMED WITH BLACK PEOPLE.

IN FEBRUARY 1962, THE FEDERAL DISTRICT JUDGE SIDNEY MIZE RULED AGAINST ME.

THE PLAINTIFF HAS NOT PROVEN THAT HE WAS DENIED ADMISSION TO THE UNIVERSITY OF MISSISSIPPI SOLELY BECAUSE OF HIS RACE. THE COMPLAINT MUST BE DENIED.

THAT JUNE, IN NEW ORLEANS, THE FIFTH CIRCUIT COURT OF APPEALS REVERSED THE LOWER COURT'S DECISION. WHILE REJECTING THE STATE'S ARGUMENT, JUDGE JOHN MINOR WISDOM SAW ME AS A MAN OF CHARACTER.

MEREDITH IS JUST ABOUT THE TYPE OF NEGRO WHO MIGHT BE EXPECTED TO CRACK THE RACIAL BARRIER AT THE UNIVERSITY OF MISSISSIPPI: A MAN WITH A MISSION AND A NERVOUS STOMACH.

BUT THE MISSISSIPPI SYSTEM OF JUSTICE WAS AT WORK TOO.

I WAS ARRESTED ON A TRUMPED-UP CHARGE OF REGISTERING TO VOTE IN ONE COUNTY WHILE LIVING IN ANOTHER. MY LAWYERS BAILED ME OUT. JAIL IS NOT MY IDEA OF THE BEST PLACE FROM WHICH TO FIGHT A WAR.

THAT SUMMER, THE MISSISSIPPI COURTS KEPT DELAYING THE ENFORCEMENT OF THE CIRCUIT COURT'S DECISION. I GOT FRUSTRATED. I COULD HAVE GRADUATED FROM JACKSON STATE COLLEGE, AND I WAS SUPPORTING MY WIFE AND CHILD. I HAD ALREADY BEEN ACCEPTED FOR GRADUATE SCHOOL PROGRAMS. BUT I KEPT ON.

IN MY HOMETOWN OF KOSCIUSKO, MOST BLACKS TREATED ME LIKE A HERO. BUT ONE BOY QUESTIONED ME.

I STILL DON'T SEE WHAT YOU EXPECT TO GAIN, EVEN IF YOU GO TO THAT SCHOOL.

I TALKED ABOUT MY GREAT WISH TO SWEEP MY PEOPLE INTO UNSTOPPABLE ACTION. THEN MY FRIEND MIKE BELL CHIMED IN.

DO YOU KNOW THE STORY OF THE MEN WHO WENT TO AFRICA TO HUNT RABBITS?

?

!!

MIKE RELATED HOW THE HUNTERS GOT OFF THEIR SHIPS, ARMED WITH GUNS AND DOGS. HE THEN DESCRIBED A WISE OLD RABBIT WHO GATHERED HIS BROTHERS AND SISTERS.

SINCE WE ARE GOING TO DIE ANYWAY, WHY BE CHASED FIRST? LET'S MARCH DOWN TO THE SEA AND DROWN OURSELVES!

THE ELEPHANTS SAW ALL THE RABBITS MARCHING TOGETHER, AND THEY SCATTERED TO THE FOUR WINDS IN FEAR OF THIS SOLIDARITY.

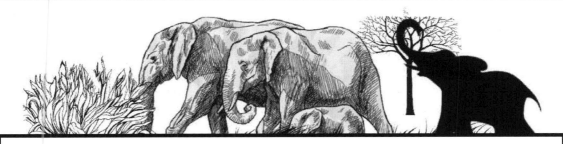

THE LIONS SAW THESE RABBITS FOLLOWING BEHIND THEIR LEADER, AND THEY DISAPPEARED INTO THE DEPTHS OF THE JUNGLE.

WHEN THE HUNTERS SAW ALL THESE RABBITS WILLING TO DIE TOGETHER, THEY THREW AWAY THEIR GUNS AND RAN FOR THEIR SHIPS.

MY FRIEND'S STORY CLARIFIED MY OWN THINKING. IT HAD A LASTING IMPACT ON ME. MORE THAN EVER, I REALIZED THAT THE SUCCESS OF MY MISSION DEPENDED ON THE SUPPORT OF MY PEOPLE.

WAIT A MINUTE. WE DON'T HAVE TO DROWN OURSELVES. ALL WE HAVE TO DO IS STICK TOGETHER!

# CHAPTER THREE:
# THE BATTLE OF OLE MISS

FOR MOST OF SEPTEMBER, I WAS STUCK IN MEMPHIS, FIRST AT MY COUSIN'S HOUSE AND THEN AT MILLINGTON NAVAL STATION.

THE FEDERAL GOVERNMENT WAS SUPPOSED TO ENFORCE MY RIGHT TO ATTEND OLE MISS, BUT MY FIRST ATTEMPT TO REGISTER IN OXFORD ON SEPTEMBER 20 SHOWED THE DEPTHS OF WHITE RESISTANCE.

ON SEPTEMBER 25, I TRIED AGAIN TO REGISTER AT A FEDERAL BUILDING IN JACKSON. ANOTHER MOB WAS WAITING.

GOVERNOR ROSS BARNETT BLOCKED ME FROM THE UNIVERSITY OFFICIALS. HE HANDED ME A SECOND PROCLAMATION DENYING MY ADMISSION.

BARNETT WAS DEFYING THE AUTHORITY OF THE FEDERAL GOVERNMENT, INCLUDING ATTORNEY GENERAL ROBERT F. KENNEDY.

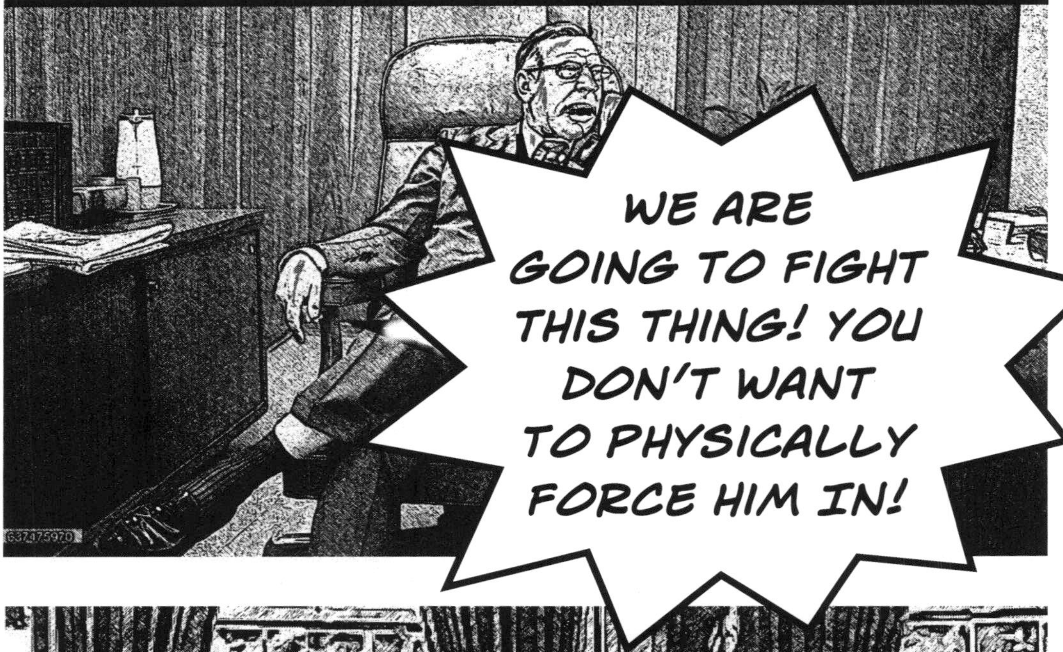
WE ARE GOING TO FIGHT THIS THING! YOU DON'T WANT TO PHYSICALLY FORCE HIM IN!

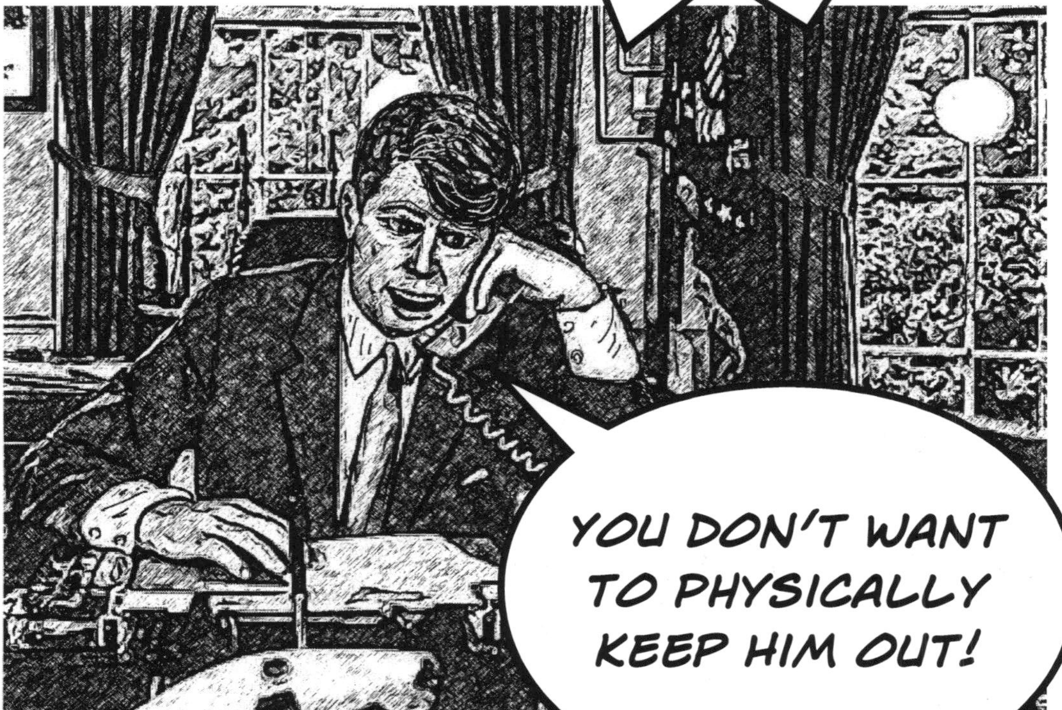
YOU DON'T WANT TO PHYSICALLY KEEP HIM OUT!

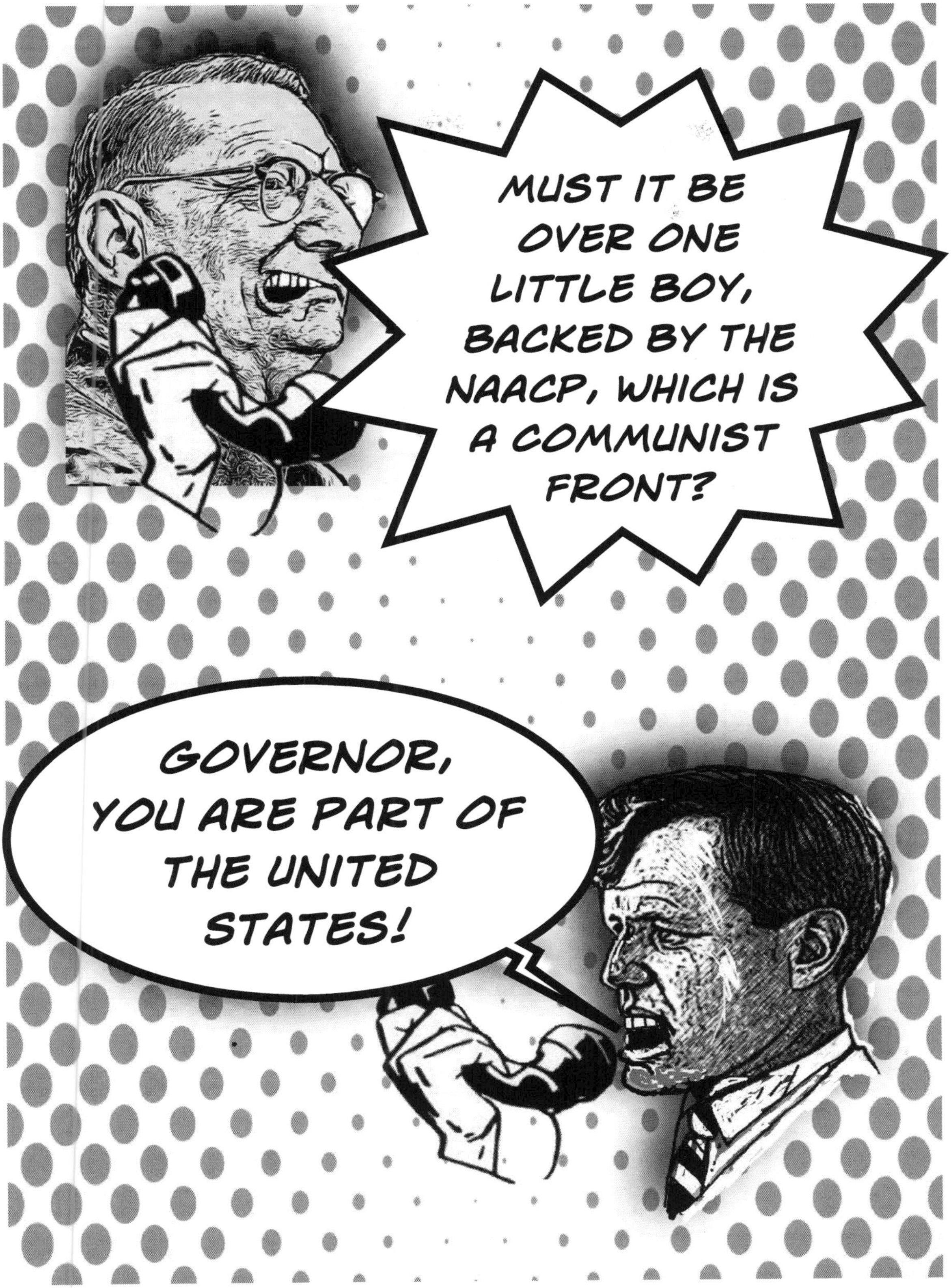
MUST IT BE OVER ONE LITTLE BOY, BACKED BY THE NAACP, WHICH IS A COMMUNIST FRONT?
GOVERNOR, YOU ARE PART OF THE UNITED STATES!

ON SEPTEMBER 26, BEFORE MY THIRD ATTEMPT TO REGISTER, I HANDED MRS. MOTLEY A STATEMENT.

The future of the United States of America, the future of the South, the future of Mississippi, and the future of the Negro rests on the decision of whether or not the Negro citizen is allowed to receive an education in his own state. If a state is permitted to arbitrarily deny any right that is so basic to the American way of life to any citizen, then democracy is a failure.

WHEN THE U.S. MARSHALS AND I ARRIVED IN OXFORD, LT. GOVERNOR PAUL JOHNSON AND STATE TROOPERS ONCE MORE BLOCKED US FROM REGISTERING.

GOVERNOR, ARE THESE MEN UNDER YOUR AUTHORITY PHYSICALLY PREVENTING US FROM GOING IN?

THEY ARE!

THE NEXT DAY, OUR CARAVAN HEADED BACK TO OXFORD FOR ANOTHER ATTEMPT.

BUT ROSS BARNETT PLEADED THAT THE MOB COULD CAUSE 100 DEATHS. BEFORE WE REACHED CAMPUS, BOBBY KENNEDY ORDERED US TO TURN BACK.

ON SATURDAY, SEPTEMBER 29, ROSS BARNETT WAS IN JACKSON FOR THE OLE MISS FOOTBALL GAME AGAINST KENTUCKY.

I LOVE MISSISSIPPI! I LOVE HER PEOPLE! I LOVE AND RESPECT OUR HERITAGE!

MY CASE WAS GOING DOWN IN HISTORY AS ONE OF THE SUPREME TESTS OF THE UNION. ON SUNDAY, SEPTEMBER 30, PRESIDENT JOHN F. KENNEDY ADDRESSED THE NATION.

OUR NATION IS FOUNDED ON THE PRINCIPLE THAT OBSERVANCE OF THE LAW IS THE ETERNAL SAFEGUARD OF LIBERTY AND DEFIANCE OF THE LAW IS THE SUREST ROAD TO TYRANNY.

THAT NIGHT WE LANDED IN OXFORD. THE AIRPORT WAS UNRECOGNIZABLE. THERE WERE FLOODLIGHTS, ROWS OF PLANES, AND HUNDREDS OF U.S. MARSHALS.

OUR CARAVAN ARRIVED AT MY DORMITORY, BAXTER HALL, WITHOUT INCIDENT. I READ A NEWSPAPER AND WENT TO BED. ALL NIGHT I HEARD GUNSHOTS.

AT THE LYCEUM BUILDING, ABOUT 2,000 PEOPLE WERE PROTESTING MY ENROLLMENT, TOSSING ROCKS AND MOLOTOV COCKTAILS. THE MARSHALS HELD THEM OFF WITH TEAR GAS.

WHEN THE NATIONAL GUARD ARRIVED THAT NIGHT, THE MOB ATTACKED WITH BRICKS AND BOTTLES.

A JOURNALIST WAS SHOT UNDER MYSTERIOUS CIRCUMSTANCES, WHILE A REPAIRMAN WAS STRUCK BY A STRAY BULLET. INSIDE THE LYCEUM, IT LOOKED LIKE A WAR ZONE, FULL OF WOUNDED SOLDIERS AND PRISONERS.

THE NEXT DAY THE CAMPUS
WAS STILL IN CHAOS.

GRADUALLY, THE TROOPS RESTORED ORDER, BUT THE DAMAGE WAS DONE.

I AWOKE ON MONDAY, OCTOBER 1, TO THE SMELL OF TEAR GAS.

I FINALLY REGISTERED AS A STUDENT AT THE UNIVERSITY OF MISSISSIPPI.

I HAD CRACKED THE WALL OF WHITE SUPREMACY. I FELT RELIEF THAT I HAD CONTRIBUTED TO THE FIGHT FOR DIGNITY. BUT I FELT NO JOY.

NOW THAT YOU ARE FINALLY REGISTERED, ARE YOU HAPPY?

THIS IS NO HAPPY OCCASION.

MY ORDEAL WAS JUST BEGINNING.

# CHAPTER FOUR:
# THE PRICE OF CITIZENSHIP

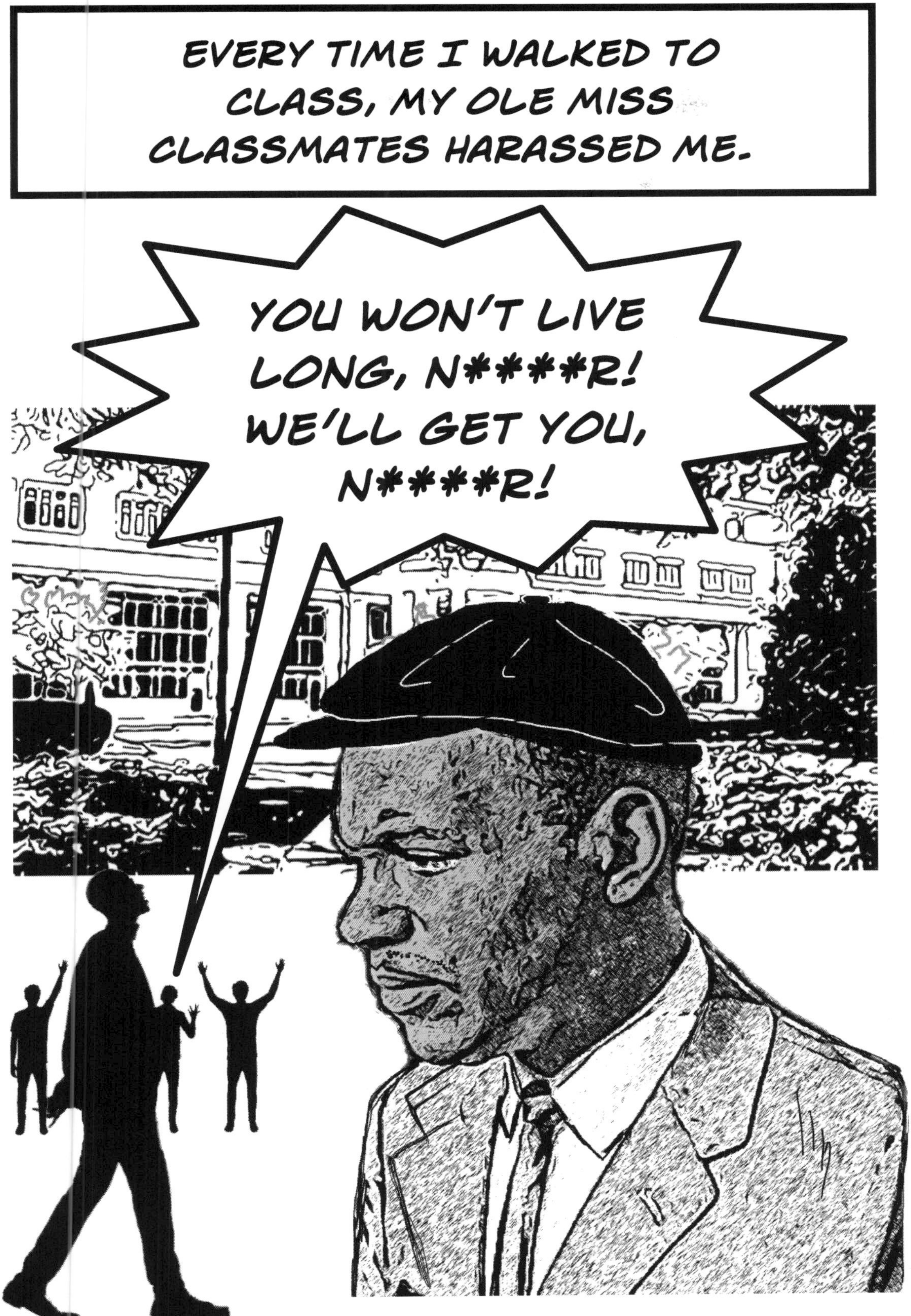
EVERY TIME I WALKED TO CLASS, MY OLE MISS CLASSMATES HARASSED ME.
YOU WON'T LIVE LONG, N****R! WE'LL GET YOU, N****R!

I WAS HANGED IN EFFIGY, AND
I RECEIVED DEATH THREATS.

ROSES ARE RED, VIOLETS ARE BLUE.
I'VE KILLED ONE N****R AND
MIGHT AS WELL KILL TWO.

ONE STUDENT IN MY DORMITORY KEPT DEFACING THE WATER FOUNTAIN.

I ALSO FOUND A DEAD RACCOON ON TOP OF MY CAR.

SOMETIMES, MY MERE PRESENCE RILED UP A MOB OF STUDENTS.

WHILE I STUDIED, STUDENTS SLAMMED DOORS, BROKE BOTTLES, AND SHOT FIRECRACKERS.

U.S. MARSHALS FLANKED
MY EVERY MOVE.

I WAS ALONE, BUT
NEVER BY MYSELF.

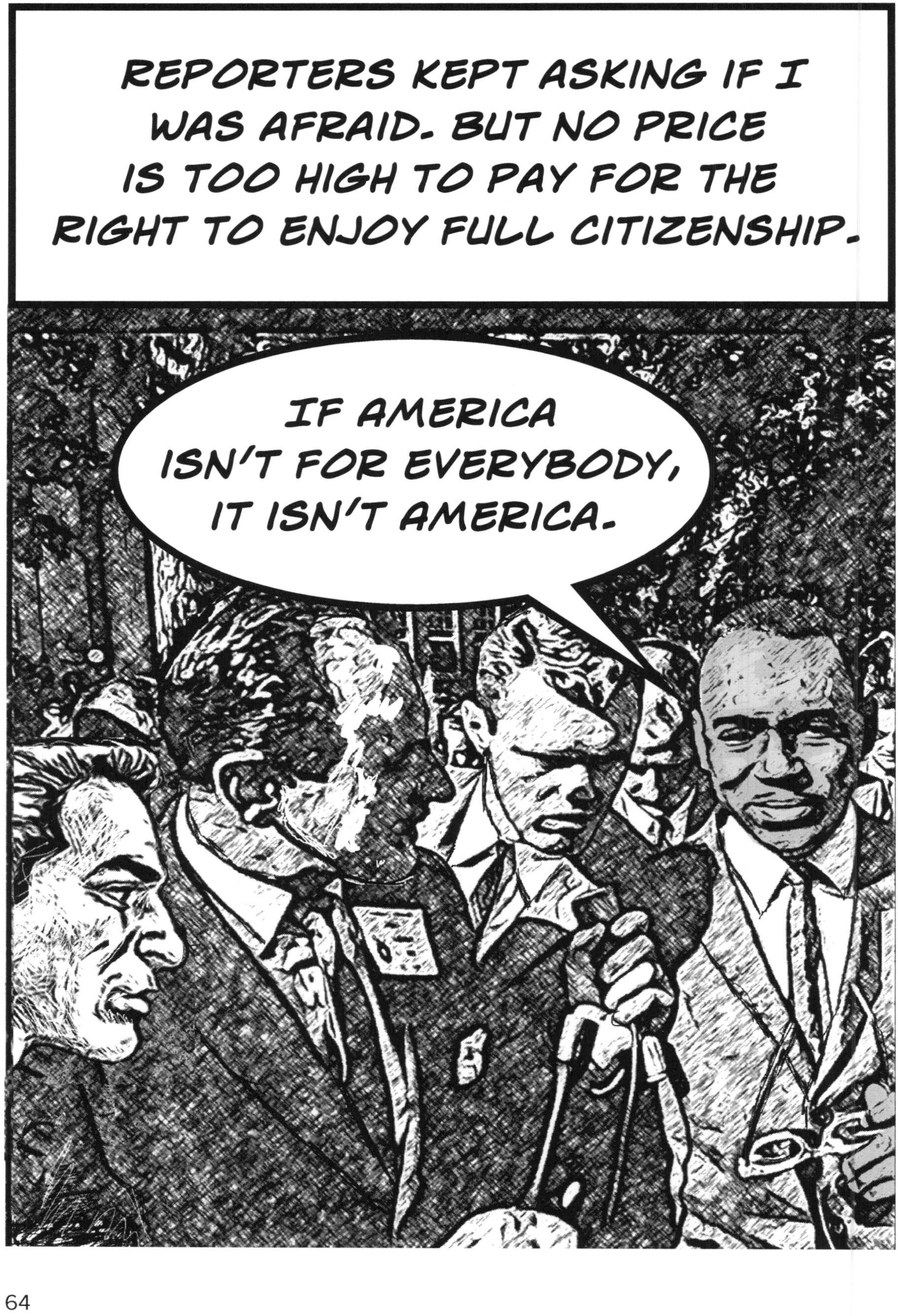
REPORTERS KEPT ASKING IF I WAS AFRAID. BUT NO PRICE IS TOO HIGH TO PAY FOR THE RIGHT TO ENJOY FULL CITIZENSHIP.
IF AMERICA ISN'T FOR EVERYBODY, IT ISN'T AMERICA.

U.S. TROOPS KEPT ORDER ON CAMPUS.
IN A SEARCH OF TWO BUILDINGS,
THEY CONFISCATED RIFLES, GASOLINE
CANS, TEAR GAS, HAND GRENADES,
AND A MACHETE.

I OBJECTED, THOUGH, THAT BLACK SOLDIERS WERE JUST SERVING ON GARBAGE TRUCKS. THEY WERE SOON INTEGRATED BACK INTO THEIR UNITS.

THIS WAS A DISHONOR AND DISGRACE TO THE HUNDREDS OF THOUSANDS OF BLACKS WHO WEAR THE UNIFORMS OF OUR MILITARY SERVICE.

OVER TIME, FEWER TROOPS WERE NECESSARY. SOME STUDENTS WERE COURTEOUS. MOST JUST IGNORED ME.

BY THE END OF FALL, I HAD SEEN THAT PEOPLE WERE AFRAID OF CHANGE. BUT WE COULD ALSO FIND COMMON GROUND.

IF YOU'RE HERE TO GET AN EDUCATION, I'M FOR YOU. IF YOU'RE HERE TO CAUSE TROUBLE, I'M AGAINST YOU.

THAT SEEMS FAIR ENOUGH TO ME.

# CHAPTER FIVE:

# THE MOST SEGREGATED MAN IN THE WORLD

DURING THE CHRISTMAS BREAK, THE NAACP ARRANGED FOR SPECIAL TUTORING AT YALE UNIVERSITY. IT WAS A FIASCO.

NOTHING THAT I WAS FIGHTING FOR WAS UP THERE— MY PEOPLE, MY FAMILY, MY FRIENDS, FREEDOM OF CHOICE, WARMTH, LOVE, CLOSENESS.

I VISITED THE COMEDIAN DICK GREGORY IN CHICAGO. HE HAD BAD NEWS FROM MISSISSIPPI.

MY SISTER, WILLIE LOU, SAID THAT BUCKSHOT HAD BEEN FIRED THROUGH ALL THE FRONT WINDOWS.

SOME WHITE FOOLS TRIED TO KILL ME! BUT I JUMPED BEHIND THE REFRIGERATOR!

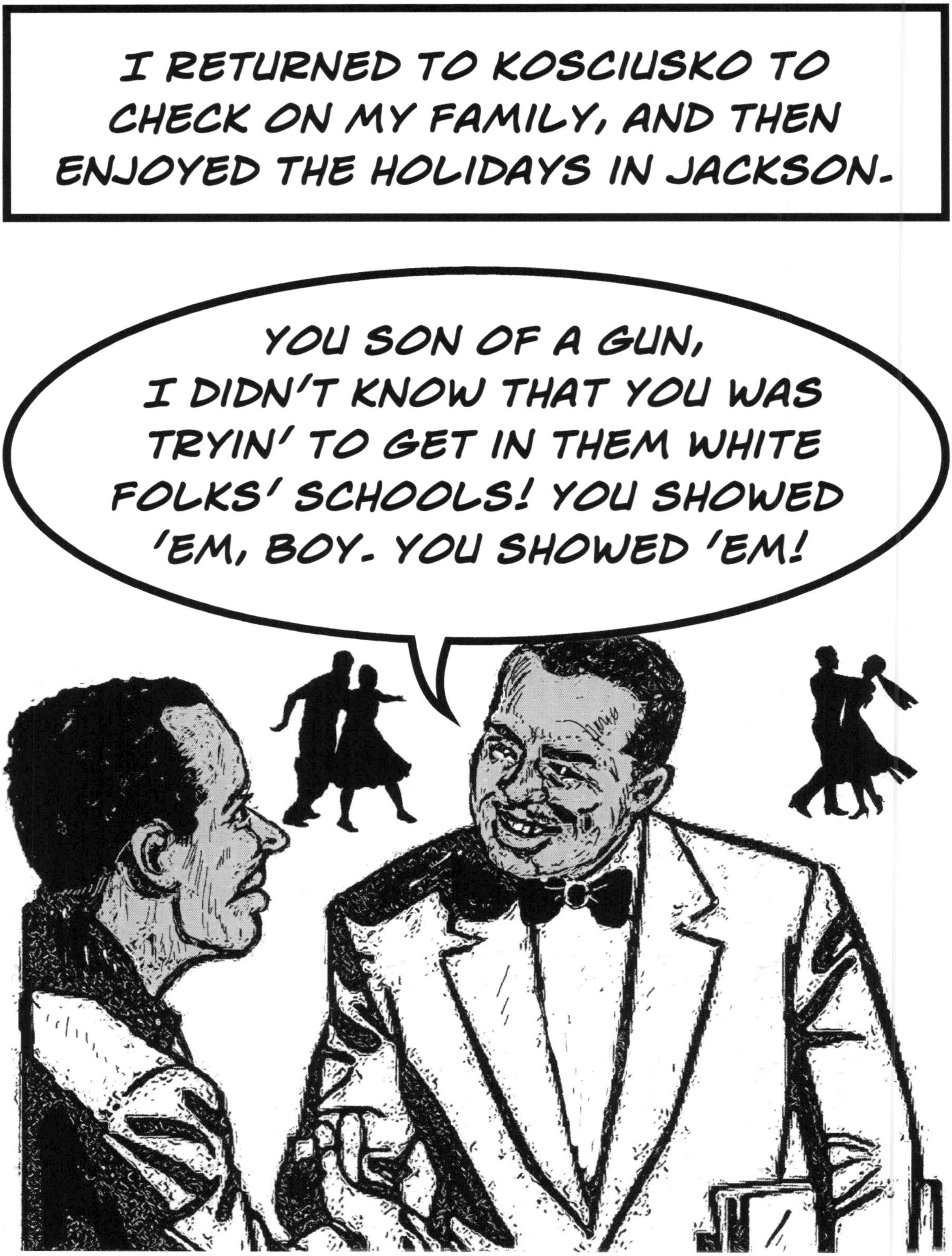
I RETURNED TO KOSCIUSKO TO CHECK ON MY FAMILY, AND THEN ENJOYED THE HOLIDAYS IN JACKSON.
YOU SON OF A GUN, I DIDN'T KNOW THAT YOU WAS TRYIN' TO GET IN THEM WHITE FOLKS' SCHOOLS! YOU SHOWED 'EM, BOY. YOU SHOWED 'EM!

ON NEW YEAR'S DAY, 1963, THE WRITER JAMES BALDWIN CAME TO VISIT. HE WAS ALWAYS OBSERVING, SOMETIMES ASKING A PROBING QUESTION. HE HAD A SHARP MIND AND A KEEN SENSE OF FEELING.

JAMES MEREDITH IS VERY GENTLE. HE'S ALSO ONE OF THE NOBLEST PEOPLE I HAVE MET.

MY WIFE MARY JUNE SUSTAINED
ME WITH HER LOVE.

OH, JAMES, I AM SO PROUD OF YOU. I WANT TO SEE YOU GET YOUR DEGREE FROM OLE MISS.

...AND MY PARENTS INSPIRED
ME WITH THEIR FAITH.

JESUS CHRIST HAD TO SUFFER, AND HE WAS THE SON OF GOD. I KNOW YOU CAN DO IT.

BACK IN OXFORD, AN UNDERGROUND STUDENT NEWSPAPER CALLED "REBEL UNDERGROUND" DEMANDED THE REMOVAL OF "KENNEDY'S FOUR-MILLION-DOLLAR COON."

JUST HAVING A BLACK MAN IN RESIDENCE DID NOT MEAN THE UNIVERSITY HAD BEEN INTEGRATED. MOST OF THE TIME, I WAS PERHAPS THE MOST SEGREGATED MAN IN THE WORLD.

I WAS AFRAID THAT IF THESE EXTRAORDINARY CONDITIONS CONTINUED THEY WOULD BECOME THE STANDARD FOR BLACK STUDENTS, SO I RELEASED A STATEMENT.

I have decided not to register during the second semester at the University of Mississippi unless very definite and positive changes are made to make my situation conducive to learning.

THE OPPOSITION SMELLED VICTORY.

CROWDS THREW ROCKS, CURSED, CHANTED, STOMPED, AND BEAT ON TABLES WITH KNIVES, FORKS, SPOONS, TRAYS, AND FISTS.

I RECEIVED SUPPORT FROM MY OWN PEOPLE. AS ONE OF MY FRIENDS PUT IT: EVERY BLACK PERSON IN AMERICA WAS IN COLLEGE.

I LEFT CAMPUS, AND EVERYONE WONDERED IF I WOULD RETURN.

ON JANUARY 30, I HELD A PRESS CONFERENCE IN JACKSON, WITH MEDGAR EVERS BY MY SIDE.

I HAVE CONCLUDED THAT THE "NEGRO" SHOULD NOT RETURN TO THE UNIVERSITY OF MISSISSIPPI. HOWEVER, I HAVE DECIDED THAT I, J.H. MEREDITH, WILL REGISTER FOR THE SECOND SEMESTER AT THE UNIVERSITY OF MISSISSIPPI.

FOR ONE SEMESTER, I HAD REPRESENTED ALL BLACK PEOPLE. NOW, I WANTED TO BE RESPECTED AS AN INDIVIDUAL.

# CHAPTER SIX:

# OUR PEOPLE'S FIGHT

WHEN I RETURNED FOR THE
SPRING SEMESTER, THERE WERE
EVEN MORE MARSHALS AND
SOLDIERS STATIONED ALL
OVER THE CAMPUS.

THE HARASSMENT NEVER STOPPED. I STILL DEALT WITH FIRECRACKERS, JOSTLING, AND HECKLERS.

BABOON! B*ST**D! COCONUT-HEADED C**N!

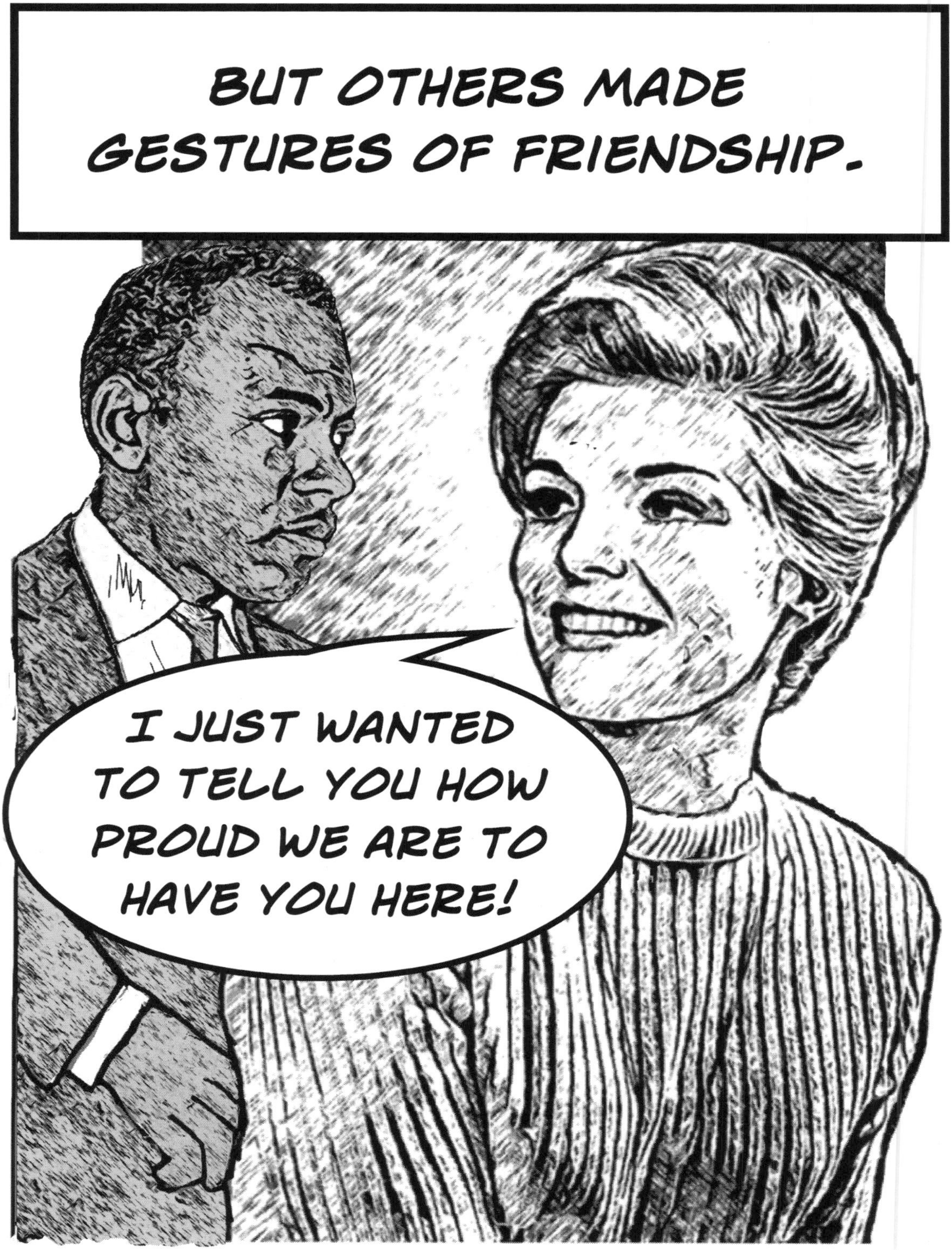
BUT OTHERS MADE GESTURES OF FRIENDSHIP.
I JUST WANTED TO TELL YOU HOW PROUD WE ARE TO HAVE YOU HERE!

WHEN THE HISTORY PROFESSOR JAMES SILVER INVITED ME TO PLAY GOLF, MARSHALS AND POLICEMEN STOOD GUARD, WHILE AN ARMY HELICOPTER CIRCLED OVERHEAD.

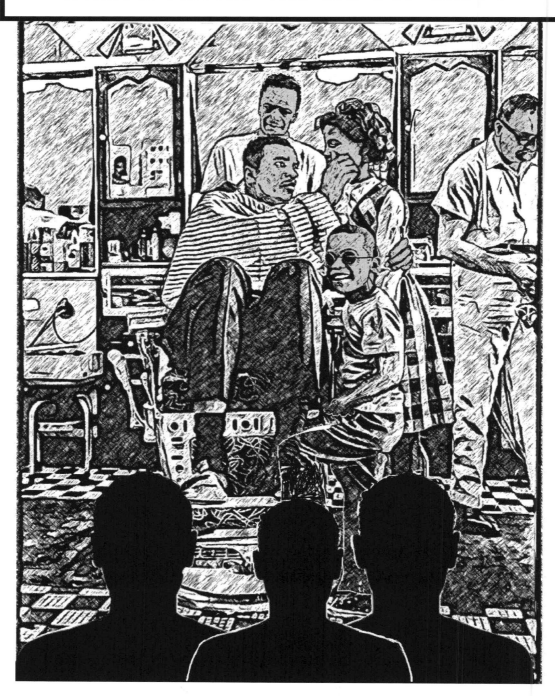

BLACKS IN OXFORD TREATED ME WITH SPECIAL WARMTH. FAMILIES INVITED ME TO DINNER. CROWDS ARRIVED WHEN I VISITED THE BARBER SHOP.

I APPEARED ON NBC'S "MEET THE PRESS." MILLIONS OF PEOPLE WATCHED ME ON TELEVISION AND HEARD ME ON THE RADIO.

HOW MUCH OF AN EDUCATION WERE YOU ABLE TO GET?

I HAVE LEARNED AN AWFUL LOT. PERHAPS MORE OUT OF THE CLASSROOM.

OUR PEOPLE'S FIGHT CONTINUED. IN JUNE 1963, WITH THE PROTECTION OF THE NATIONAL GUARD, JAMES HOOD AND VIVIAN MALONE INTEGRATED THE UNIVERSITY OF ALABAMA.

SEGREGATION IS BREAKING DOWN. WE HAVE SHOWN THAT IT CAN BE DONE.

FOR THE SUMMER SESSION AT OLE MISS, I HAD A NEW ROOMMATE. CLEVE MCDOWELL HAD BEEN ADMITTED TO LAW SCHOOL.

BUT AFTER I GRADUATED AND THE MARSHALS LEFT, CLEVE FEARED FOR HIS LIFE WHILE WALKING TO CLASSES. THAT FALL, HE GOT EXPELLED FOR CARRYING A GUN.

IN JUNE, MY FRIEND MEDGAR EVERS WAS ASSASSINATED. IT DEVASTATED ME. I RELEASED A BITTER STATEMENT TO THE MEDIA.

NOTHING IS PROVIDED UNDER THIS SYSTEM FOR THE NEGRO THAT IS WORTH HAVING. WE CAN, WE MUST, AND WE WILL CHANGE THIS SYSTEM.

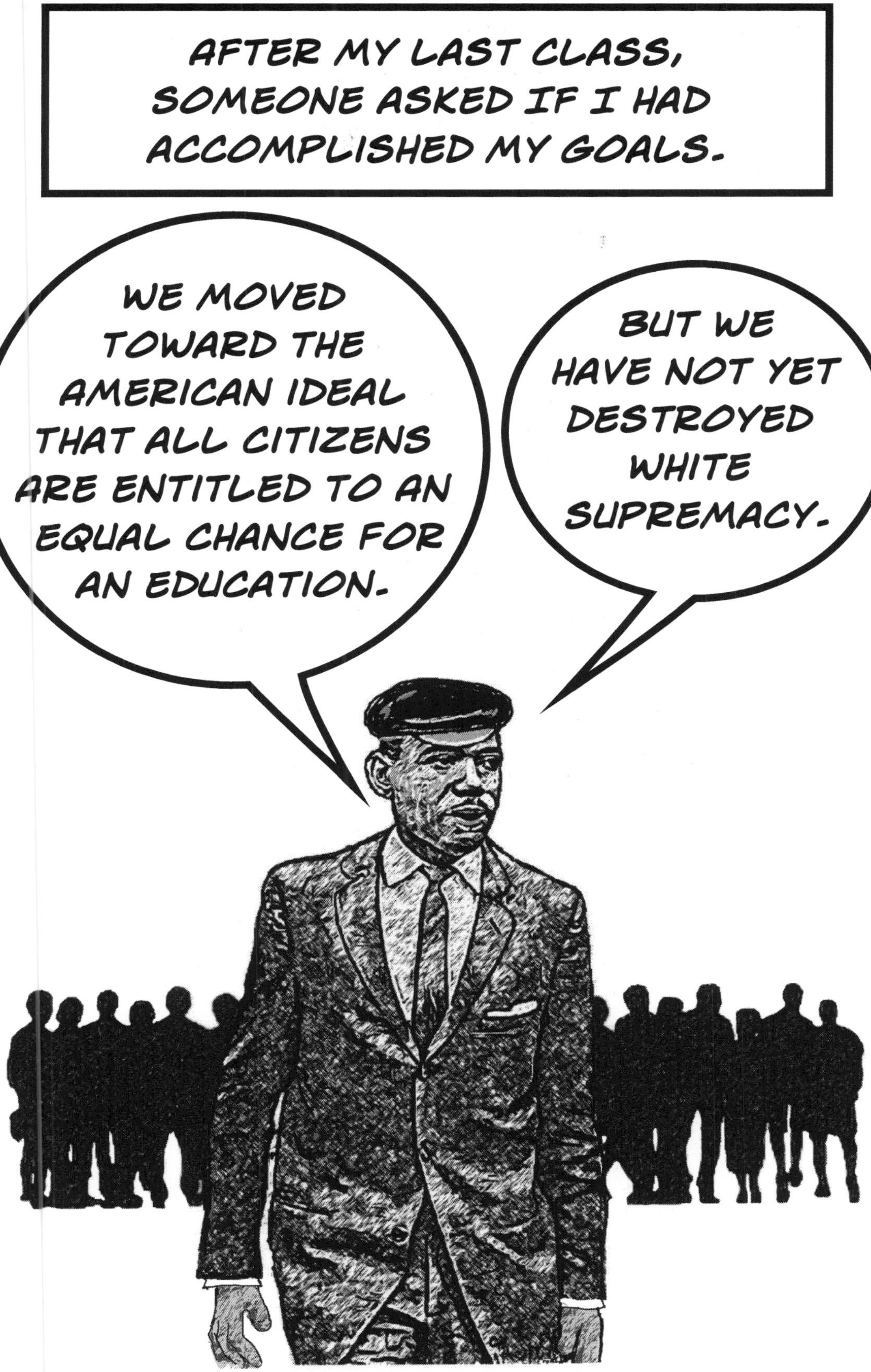
AFTER MY LAST CLASS, SOMEONE ASKED IF I HAD ACCOMPLISHED MY GOALS.
WE MOVED TOWARD THE AMERICAN IDEAL THAT ALL CITIZENS ARE ENTITLED TO AN EQUAL CHANCE FOR AN EDUCATION.
BUT WE HAVE NOT YET DESTROYED WHITE SUPREMACY.

ON AUGUST 19, 1963, I GRADUATED FROM THE UNIVERSITY OF MISSISSIPPI.

WE MARCHED PAST THE CONFEDERATE STATUE, A SYMBOL OF WHITE SUPREMACY.

MY FATHER NEVER EXPECTED TO SEE ME ON THIS DAY. MY YOUNG SON WAS STILL UNAWARE OF WHITE SUPREMACY.

THIS BATTLE WAS OVER.

BUT THE WAR CONTINUED.

# CHAPTER SEVEN: MY OWN WAY

NOW I WAS A CIVIL RIGHTS HERO. BUT I NEVER REALLY FIT IN THE MOVEMENT. AT THE NAACP'S CONVENTION, I CHIDED THEIR YOUNG ACTIVISTS.

I AM MOST SADLY STRUCK BY THE INEFFECTIVENESS OF OUR NEGRO YOUTH LEADERS.

I WAS TOO INDEPENDENT TO JOIN ANY CIVIL RIGHTS ORGANIZATION. I SOUGHT MY OWN WAY.

I MOVED TO WASHINGTON, D.C., AND TRIED TO START AN EDUCATION FUND FOR BLACK STUDENTS.

I SPENT A YEAR STUDYING AT THE UNIVERSITY OF IBADAN IN NIGERIA.

I GRADUATED FROM COLUMBIA UNIVERSITY LAW SCHOOL.

I PUBLISHED A MEMOIR ABOUT THE BATTLE OF OLE MISS.

JAMES MEREDITH

THREE YEARS IN **MISSISSIPPI**

IN 1966, I STARTED A WALK THROUGH MISSISSIPPI, ENCOURAGING BLACK PEOPLE TO DEFY RACIST INTIMIDATION BY REGISTERING TO VOTE.

ON THE SECOND DAY, I WAS SHOT.

THOUSANDS OF PEOPLE CONTINUED THE MEREDITH MARCH AGAINST FEAR. AS BLACK FOLKS IN MISSISSIPPI REGISTERED TO VOTE, STOKELY CARMICHAEL INTRODUCED THE SLOGAN OF BLACK POWER.

I RECUPERATED FROM MY WOUNDS AND JOINED THE FINAL STRETCH OF THE MARCH INTO JACKSON, WALKING ALONGSIDE MARTIN LUTHER KING.

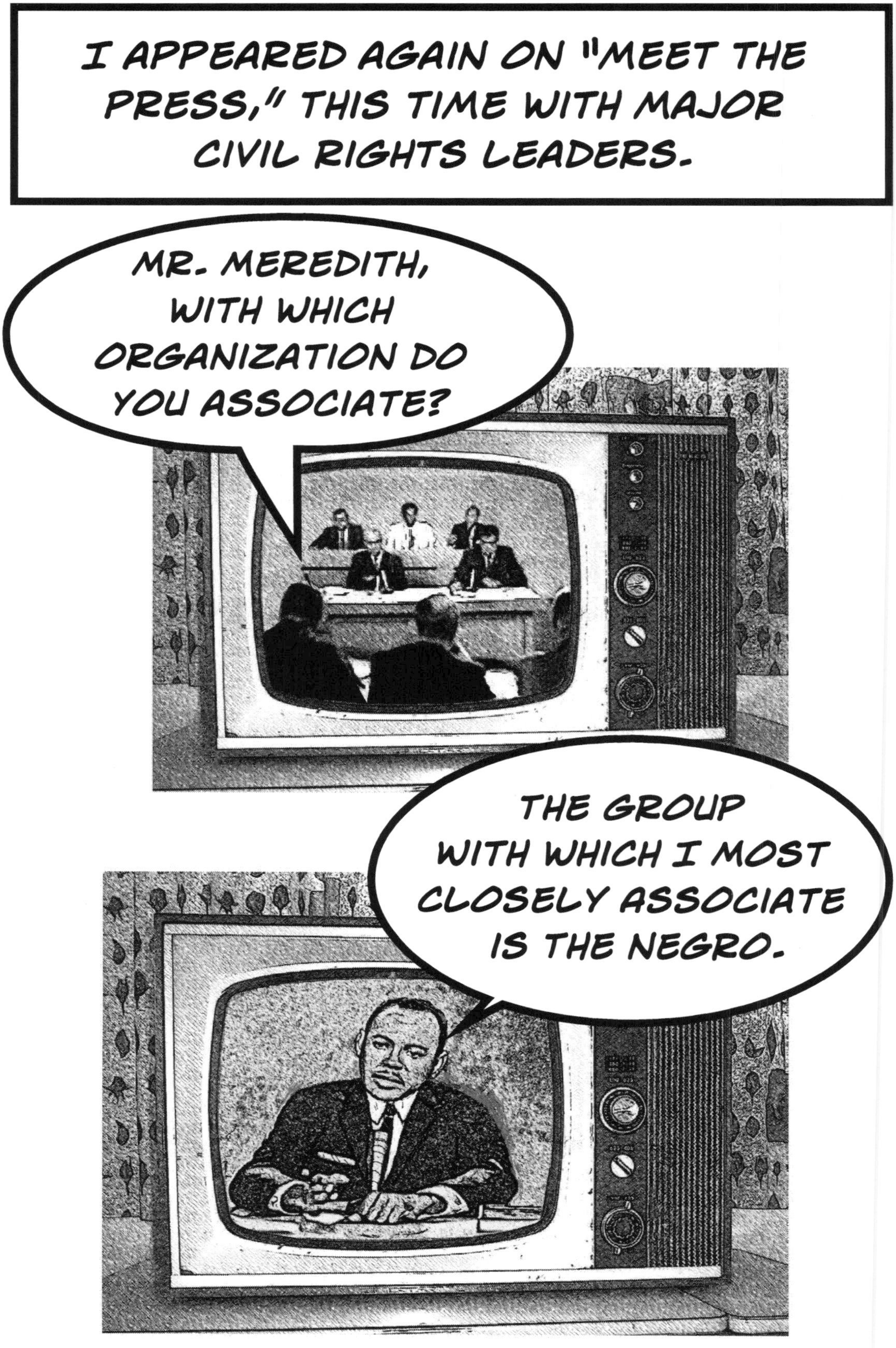
I APPEARED AGAIN ON "MEET THE PRESS," THIS TIME WITH MAJOR CIVIL RIGHTS LEADERS.
MR. MEREDITH, WITH WHICH ORGANIZATION DO YOU ASSOCIATE?
THE GROUP WITH WHICH I MOST CLOSELY ASSOCIATE IS THE NEGRO.

IN 1967, I RAN AS A REPUBLICAN AGAINST THE LONGTIME DEMOCRATIC CONGRESSMAN FROM NEW YORK, ADAM CLAYTON POWELL.

BUT THE PEOPLE OF HARLEM WERE ANGRY THAT I WAS CHALLENGING THEIR POLITICAL HERO, AND I DROPPED OUT OF THE RACE.

SOMETIMES I CONFUSE PEOPLE. IN 1967, WHEN MY OLD ENEMY ROSS BARNETT RAN FOR GOVERNOR AGAIN, I ENDORSED HIM. I REALLY THOUGHT HE HAD THE BEST CHANCE TO LIFT UP MISSISSIPPI.

EVEN BARNETT WAS CONFUSED. HE THOUGHT I WAS TRYING TO SABOTAGE HIM WITH WHITE VOTERS!

BY THE 1970s, I HAD MOVED BACK
TO MISSISSIPPI, WHERE I OWNED
DIFFERENT BUSINESSES.

I ALSO RAN FOR PUBLIC OFFICE—
AS A DEMOCRAT, REPUBLICAN, AND
INDEPENDENT. I NEVER WON.

IN THE 1980s, I MOVED TO CINCINNATI AND THEN WASHINGTON, D.C. AT TIMES, I WAS CONTROVERSIAL—ESPECIALLY WHEN I ASSOCIATED WITH RIGHT-WING POLITICIANS.

BUT I HAVE ALWAYS KEPT A STRONG CONSERVATIVE STREAK. MY LIFE REPRESENTS THE POWER OF INDIVIDUALS TO MAKE THEIR OWN WAY.

FEW PEOPLE REALLY UNDERSTAND ME. I KNOW THAT I MAKE IT DIFFICULT. I DON'T CONFORM TO PEOPLE'S EXPECTATIONS OF A CIVIL RIGHTS HERO.

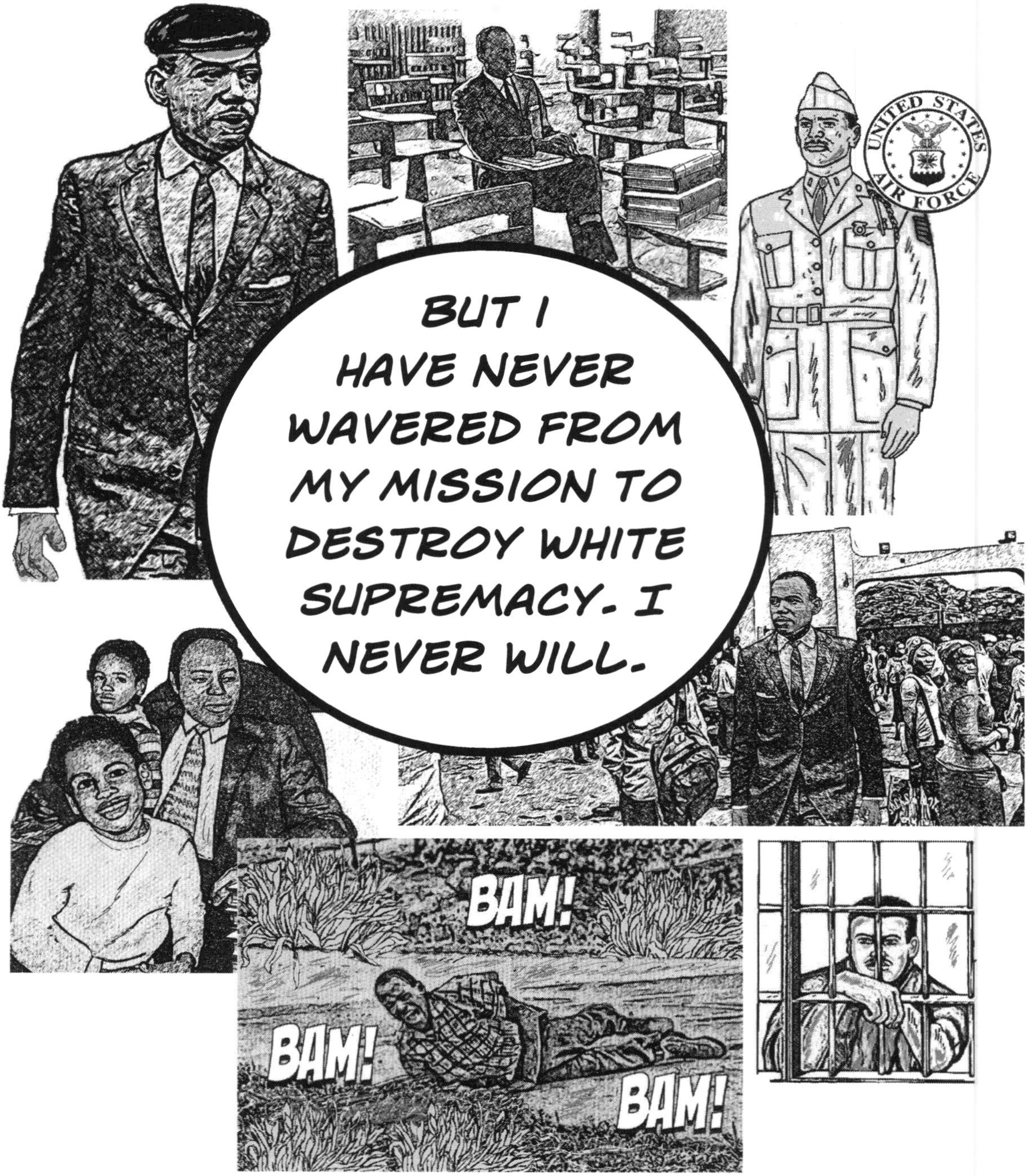
UNITED STATES AIR FORCE
BUT I HAVE NEVER WAVERED FROM MY MISSION TO DESTROY WHITE SUPREMACY. I NEVER WILL.
BAM!
BAM!
BAM!

# *EPILOGUE*

I STILL BELIEVE THAT EDUCATION CAN DESTROY WHITE SUPREMACY.

IN 2002, I WATCHED MY SON JOSEPH WIN A TOP HONOR WHILE OBTAINING A PH.D. FROM OLE MISS. I HAD FULFILLED ONE PART OF MY DIVINE MISSION.

NOW, PEOPLE THINK OF ME AS PART OF HISTORY. OLE MISS ERECTED A STATUE OF ME. BUT IT DOESN'T DESCRIBE MY FIGHT AGAINST WHITE SUPREMACY.

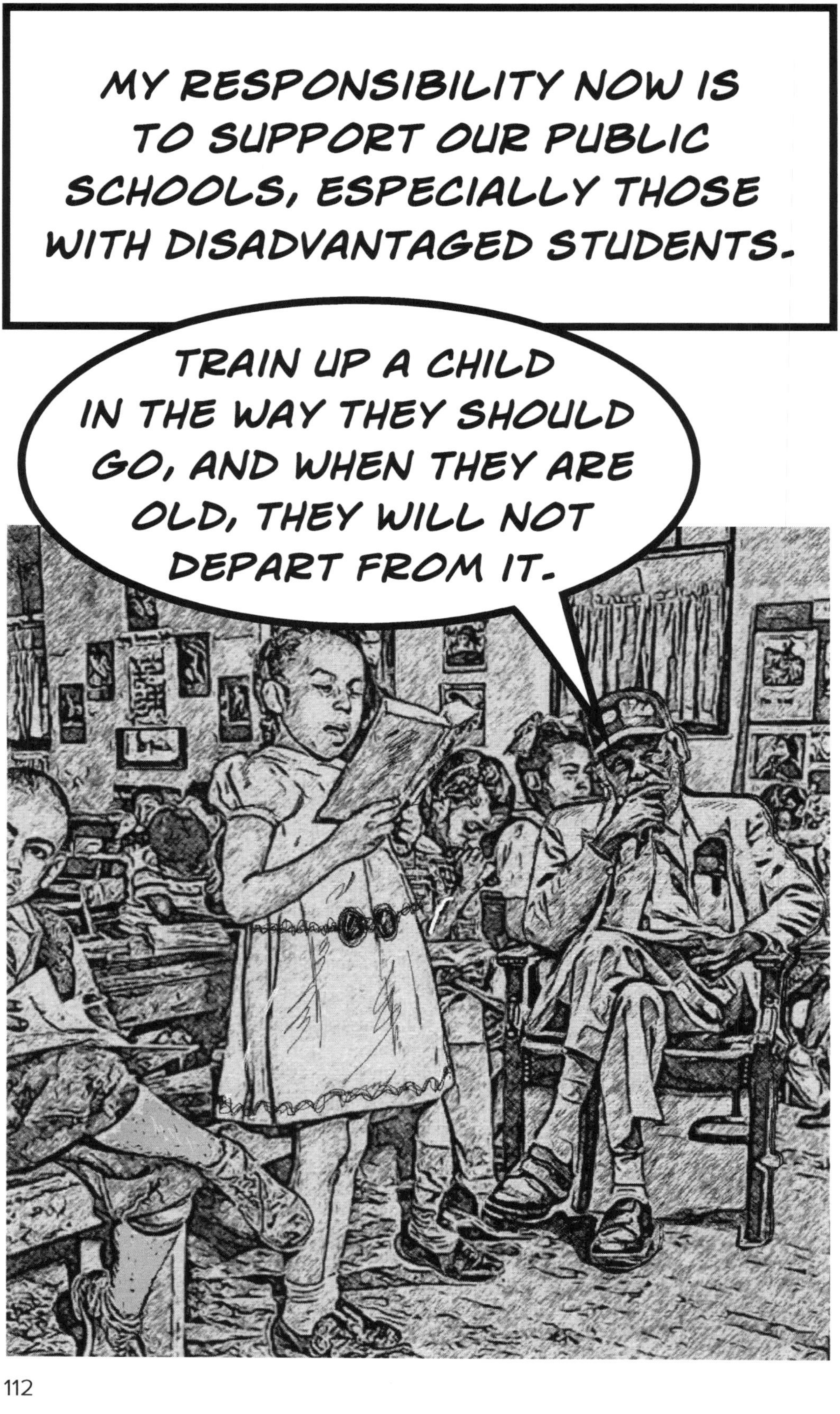
MY RESPONSIBILITY NOW IS TO SUPPORT OUR PUBLIC SCHOOLS, ESPECIALLY THOSE WITH DISADVANTAGED STUDENTS.
TRAIN UP A CHILD IN THE WAY THEY SHOULD GO, AND WHEN THEY ARE OLD, THEY WILL NOT DEPART FROM IT.

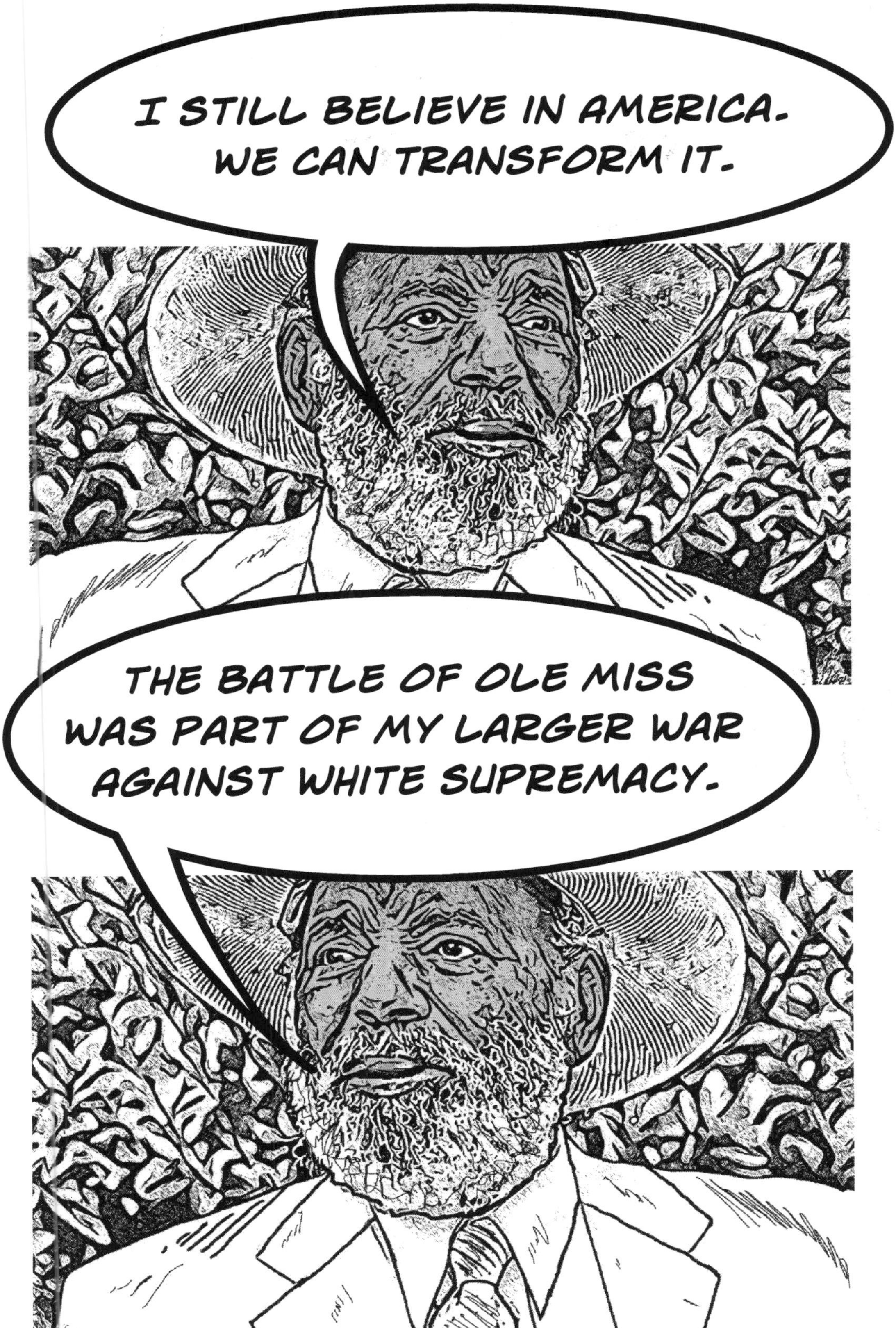
I STILL BELIEVE IN AMERICA. WE CAN TRANSFORM IT.
THE BATTLE OF OLE MISS WAS PART OF MY LARGER WAR AGAINST WHITE SUPREMACY.

THAT WAR CONTINUES. IT DEPENDS, MORE THAN EVER, ON THE NEXT GENERATION.

AS FOR ME,
I FIGHT IN MY OWN WAY.

I KNOW THAT I HAVE NOT
FULFILLED MY DIVINE MISSION.
BUT I AIN'T DEAD YET.

# DISCUSSION QUESTIONS

1. How did James Meredith's early life shape his values and politics?

2. Why did Meredith apply to the University of Mississippi?

3. Why was education important to the civil rights movement?

4. What led up to the Battle of Ole Miss? Why did it happen?

5. As Meredith sought to integrate the university, what was the role of the federal government? What was the role of the media?

6. After enrollment, what was Meredith's experience on campus? Why did he consider leaving?

7. How would you describe Meredith's political outlook? How did his views shape his activities after graduation from Ole Miss?

8. Why did Meredith begin the March against Fear in 1966? What did it accomplish?

9. Why did Meredith associate himself with a few extreme conservatives in the 1980s and 1990s?

10. What does Meredith's story mean for us today?

# THE MAKING OF *MAN ON A MISSION*

*Man on a Mission* is a work of collaboration. Aram Goudsouzian, a civil rights historian at the University of Memphis, wrote the script. Bill Murray, an illustrator whose work has appeared in a variety of national publications, drew the panels. Vijay Shah offered constant input, kept the team on task, and maintained communication with Mr. Meredith.

At times, our book posed quite a challenge. If you know James Meredith, then you know that he refuses to play the conventional role of a civil rights hero. He is an independent man. He has his own singular style. In *Man on a Mission*, we try to tell Meredith's story from his own vantage point, while putting it into an accessible, attractive graphic format.

This essay explains how we framed the story of James Meredith. We drew from Meredith's own writings, from books about the Battle of Ole Miss, and from the extensive scholarship on civil rights in Mississippi.

## The Man Himself: James Meredith

In constructing this book, we relied especially on *Three Years in Mississippi*, Meredith's memoir about his fight to attend the University of Mississippi. That book was originally published in 1966. Because Meredith wrote the book in the aftermath of the Ole Miss crisis, it captures his direct voice during this tumultuous period in American history.

*Three Years in Mississippi* reveals a man who is determined and proud. "One must always remember that I returned to my home state to fight a war," declares Meredith. When he describes his upbringing in Kosciusko, he conveys his values of independence, discipline, and education. Upon his return to Mississippi at the dawn of the 1960s, Meredith was determined to fulfill his "divine responsibility." He sought to destroy the state's system of white supremacy. In his memoir, he describes the harassment from police officers, the violence and fear faced by Black Americans, and the numerous ways that a racist society kept Black people from economic progress.

James Meredith planned to integrate the University of Mississippi because he wanted the full respect due any person. He also sought to crack the fortress of white supremacy. Ole Miss was the premier institution of higher education for white people in Mississippi. There are moments in *Three Years in Mississippi* where Meredith describes his quest with emotional, haunting language. There are other moments where he is factual and technical. These shifts in tone are part of Meredith's personality, and we try to relay this style in *Man on a Mission*.

When Meredith enrolled at Ole Miss, he called it a "supreme test of the Union." He was forcing the federal government to protect his civil rights as an American. President John F. Kennedy and his brother, attorney general Robert F. Kennedy, had focused most of their attention on the international events of the Cold War. But the mob violence in Oxford on September 30 and October 1 of 1962 generated a great deal of media coverage. It forced the Kennedy administration to pay attention. The story held significance around the world: The Cold War dominated international politics, and people worldwide read and watched the news from Mississippi, including those citizens in the newly independent nations in Africa. Did the United States really promote democracy? The Battle of Ole Miss stoked that debate.

In his own memoir, Meredith concentrates on his personal role. He braved the constant threats and insults of hostile students. He endured racist questions about his academic abilities. He survived the isolation of integrating an all-white institution. And Meredith kept trying to shape his own destiny: when he threatened not to return for the spring semester, and when he issued statements upon the assassination of Medgar Evers, he was reminding the public about his individual perspective and his personal mission.

After *Three Years in Mississippi*, Meredith did not stop writing. He is the author of a variety of self-published works, including reflections for his grandchildren, an oral history conducted by Yasuhiro Katagiri, and a book called *James Meredith vs. Ole Miss*. Notably, he collaborated with William Doyle on *A Mission from God*. This new memoir, which was published in 2012, captures Meredith's unique outlook. It incorporates details about the integration of the University of Mississippi, while also carrying Meredith's tale beyond his graduation from Ole Miss.

Today, a historian interested in Meredith's story can not only read his published books, but also conduct research in the James Howard Meredith Collection, which is located at the Department of Archives and

Special Collections at the University of Mississippi. There are 146 boxes filled with Meredith's documents, including family records, personal letters, business files, and legal papers. The University of Mississippi also holds many archival collections related to its integration, including papers from university professors, journalists, and photographers.

## Conflict on Campus: The Battle of Ole Miss

During his year at the University of Mississippi, Meredith became an important figure in American public life. Television news segments highlighted his personal ordeal. Reporters from national magazines admired him as a patriotic, determined man. He received an extraordinary amount of mail—some of it filled with hate, but much of it celebrating his courage. When Meredith graduated in August 1963, the *Chicago Defender* lauded him: "It was an ordeal that tested not only his moral character, but his mental fiber as well. American education, in all its turbulent history, has not had a comparable stalwart example."

Of course, Meredith was not the only person to write books about his moment in the spotlight. The Battle of Ole Miss was a major flashpoint in the civil rights movement of the 1960s, and it has attracted considerable attention from scholars and journalists. We learned a great deal from these accounts. In *Man on a Mission*, we incorporated details or dialogue from certain selections.

In 1965, Russell Barrett, a professor of political science at the University of Mississippi, published the first book-length treatment, entitled *Integration at Ole Miss*. That same year, Walter Lord, the author of popular books about military history and the sinking of the *Titanic*, published his own vibrant account of the Ole Miss crisis, entitled *The Past That Would Not Die*.

More recently, popular writers have introduced the Ole Miss crisis to modern readers. In *The Band Played Dixie*, Nadine Cohodas remembers the university's integration while reporting on the campus thirty-five years later. In *An American Insurrection*, William Doyle delivers a blow-by-blow narrative history of the negotiations and conflicts during Meredith's tenure at the University of Mississippi, while employing primary sources that were not available in the 1960s, such as FBI records and audio recordings from the White House. Paul Hendrickson's *Sons of Mississippi* is an especially absorbing book. It tells the story of seven white sheriffs in a famous photograph from Ole Miss in 1962, as well as the tale of Meredith and his son Joe. Relying on deep interviews, Hendrickson thoughtfully meditates on race, history, and life in Mississippi.

Other books lend unique perspectives on the conflict. For example, Kathleen Wickham's *We Believed We Were Immortal* discusses the experiences and reporting of twelve journalists who covered the violence in Oxford. Henry Gallagher's *James Meredith and the Ole Miss Riot* offers a first-person account from an army lieutenant who was on duty during Meredith's time on campus.

Academic historians have also analyzed this significant moment in civil rights history. In *The Battle of Ole Miss,* Frank Lambert places Meredith and his classmates in historical perspective, emphasizing the distinct experiences of young Mississippians across the racial divide. Lambert—who was also the punter on the 1962 Ole Miss football team—provides a short and clear history, geared especially to undergraduate college students.

By contrast, Charles Eagles has contributed a long, thorough, definitive history of the Ole Miss crisis. *The Price of Defiance* is divided into three parts. The first section describes the conservative culture at the University of Mississippi prior to the 1960s, including one chapter on the tragic story of Clennon King, who was committed to a psychiatric hospital after attempting to enter Ole Miss in 1958. The second section concentrates on Meredith's upbringing, education, and legal battle to integrate the university; Eagles aptly describes Meredith as a "militant conservative." The final section details the political maneuvering and violence that accompanied Meredith's arrival in Oxford, as well as his experiences as a student during the 1962–63 academic year. In making *Man on a Mission*, we particularly relied on *The Price of Defiance* for context and specifics about the Battle of Ole Miss.


## At the Grassroots: Civil Rights in Mississippi

In his mind, James Meredith stands apart from the civil rights movement. The Black freedom struggle was a collective crusade for social justice, but Meredith always saw himself as an individual.

Yet Meredith might be the most significant single figure in Mississippi's push for racial justice. In 1962, when he forced his way into the state's premier all-white university, he provoked a crisis for the state's politicians, especially governor Ross Barnett. Like the Freedom

Rides and other events of the civil rights movement, Meredith's challenge revealed both the determined resilience of Black activists and the violent resistance of white supremacists.

Moreover, as his own story reveals, Meredith depended on a larger Black community. We cannot understand James Meredith or the Ole Miss crisis if we do not recognize the larger contours of Black life and the civil rights movement in Mississippi.

His parents, Cap and Roxie Meredith, instilled the values of education and independence because they were protecting their son from the horrors of Jim Crow. As historian Neil McMillen describes, white Mississippians instituted a racial system in the 1890s and the early twentieth century that included restrictions on Black voting, codes of social interaction that reinforced white supremacy, and brutal violence against Black Americans. A society built on racial oppression persisted into James Meredith's adult years in the 1950s and 1960s, and its consequences fester into the present day.

The murder of Emmett Till put a spotlight on white supremacy in Mississippi. In 1954, the fourteen-year-old boy, visiting from Chicago, perhaps flirted with a white woman in a Delta convenience store. The woman's husband and brother-in-law soon seized Till, tortured him, killed him, and dumped him in a river. At a subsequent trial, the men were found innocent, and Black Americans nationwide protested the injustice. In recent years, the historians Devery Anderson, Elliott Gorn, Dave Tell, and Timothy Tyson have taken distinct approaches to telling Till's story, but together, they reinforce how this brutal, tragic murder helped birth the modern civil rights movement.

The Till murder, which occurred in the aftermath of the Supreme Court's *Brown v. Board of Education* decision, intensified white resistance to racial integration. Charles Bolton documents the long struggle to integrate Mississippi schools, with some vivid descriptions of violent white resistance. Mississippi was also home to the Citizens' Council, which was formed in 1954; as Neil McMillen describes, the organization served as a key institution in defense of segregation. Furthermore, Mississippi instituted a State Sovereignty Commission. Both Jenny Irons and Yasuhiro Katagiri document how this official state organization promoted segregationist politics and spied on activists who fought for Black freedom. In the early 1960s, the Sovereignty Commission kept a thick file on Meredith.

Yet while Meredith was in the U.S. Air Force during the 1950s,

Mississippi organizers were building Black political networks, laying a foundation for a genuine civil rights movement. Many were World War II veterans, such as Medgar Evers, Amzie Moore, and Aaron Henry. In the early 1960s, activists from the Student Nonviolent Coordinating Committee, including Bob Moses, arrived in Mississippi. They allied with local Mississippians to build community support for political action, seeking to register voters and gain political power. Michael Vinson Williams has written a fine biography of Evers, and Eric Burner has done the same for Moses.

John Dittmer's *Local People*, published in 1994, and Charles Payne's *I've Got the Light of Freedom*, published in 1995, explain the grassroots movement for Black freedom in Mississippi. Dittmer's book is a more straightforward history, beginning after World War II and continuing to the late 1960s. Payne's work is more sociological, examining the mechanics of grassroots organizing and the personal networks upon which it depended. Both books are deeply researched and creatively conceived, and together, they helped shift the entire direction of civil rights studies.

The next generation of scholars built on the insights of Dittmer and Payne. No longer could the civil rights movement be defined just through the big national flashpoints like the March on Washington (or the Ole Miss crisis) or just through major figures such as Martin Luther King Jr. (or Meredith). Scholars of local freedom movements in Mississippi—including Emilye Crosby, Françoise Hamlin, Tiyi Morris, Todd Moye, M. J. O'Brien, and Akinyele Umoja—reveal the importance of grassroots activists, especially women, and show that few Black Americans practiced nonviolence in the vein of Martin Luther King Jr. They also view a "long civil rights movement" that stretched back before World War II and continued beyond the 1960s.

By spotlighting the life of the grassroots organizer Fannie Lou Hamer, biographers Chana Kai Lee, Kay Mills, and Chris Myers Asch further this same understanding of the Mississippi movement. Other authors have focused on the 1964 Freedom Summer, including the sociologist Doug McAdam, the religious scholar Charles Marsh, and the popular writer Bruce Watson. During that summer, hundreds of volunteers traveled to Mississippi to register voters and conduct Freedom Schools. Three civil rights workers were murdered in Philadelphia, Mississippi, and civil rights organizers founded their own Mississippi Freedom Democratic Party (MFDP) when the "regular" Democratic Party blocked Black registrants. At the Democratic National Convention in 1964, the party tried to offer a compromise of two at-large delegates from the MFDP. "We didn't come all this way for two seats!" objected Hamer.

It is important to place James Meredith in this broad context. He did not spend time building consensus with local activists. He did not try to register voters or participate in demonstrations. He was very much an individualist, and he did not deem his quest to integrate the University of Mississippi as part of the grassroots-organizing tradition. Yet the Battle of Ole Miss—like local voter registration drives, Freedom Rides, and sit-ins—shaped the larger civil rights struggle in Mississippi.

In June of 1966, Meredith's efforts once again intersected with the civil rights movement. He began a walk from Memphis, Tennessee, to Jackson, Mississippi, to encourage Black voter registration and to defy white racist intimidation. In typical style, Meredith acted without consulting anyone else, though a few people accompanied him. But, on the second day, a white man shot and wounded Meredith. While he recovered, his walk turned into a mass march featuring Martin Luther King Jr. and thousands of participants. Stokely Carmichael, the new chairman of SNCC, introduced the slogan of "Black Power," which helped define the next stage of the Black freedom struggle. A recuperated Meredith joined the march's final stretch into Jackson and won huge cheers at a rally outside the state capitol. In Aram Goudsouzian's book about the Meredith March against Fear, the author paints the march as a central moment in the Black freedom struggle of the 1960s. It all began with the singular James Meredith.

As the Mississippi movement developed, white resistance evolved. Historians Joseph Crespino and Robert Luckett explain that once massive resistance became untenable, white politicians in Mississippi adopted new strategies of "strategic accommodation" that informed the politics of the New Right, while Frank Parker and Chris Danielson document the growing Black electorate and new forms of white resistance in Mississippi politics since the passage of the 1965 Voting Rights Act.

## The Struggle Continues

Just as the story of race in Mississippi does not end in the 1960s, neither does the story of Meredith. When he returned to Mississippi and ran for office in the 1970s, he operated in a new political environment. There were more Black voters, but also a tight white grip on political power. When Meredith controversially associated himself with archconservative leaders such as Jesse Helms in the 1980s, the New Right was selling itself as "colorblind."

Meanwhile, James Meredith keeps evolving. "I am George Floyd," he proclaimed in the summer of 2020, in the aftermath of a police officer's murder of the Minnesota man. As protests spread nationwide, he aligned himself with the Black Lives Matter movement. "I am filled with both joy and hope," he says. "White supremacy may be the most evil beast that's ever stalked the halls of history, and today it may finally be mortally wounded." Meredith had struck his first blow against that beast in 1962, when he stepped onto the campus of the University of Mississippi. In his own particular way, he has never given up the fight. He is still a man on a mission.

# BIBLIOGRAPHY

Anderson, Devery S. *Emmett Till: The Murder That Shocked the World and Propelled the Civil Rights Movement*. Jackson: University Press of Mississippi, 2015.

Asch, Chris Myers. *The Senator and the Sharecropper: The Freedom Struggles of James O. Eastland and Fannie Lou Hamer*. New York: The New Press, 2008.

Barrett, Russell H. *Integration at Ole Miss*. Chicago: Quadrangle Books, 1965.

Bristow, Nancy K. *Steeped in the Blood of Racism: Black Power, Law and Order, and the 1970 Shootings at Jackson State College*. New York: Oxford University Press, 2020.

Bolton, Charles C. *The Hardest Deal of All: The Battle Over School Integration in Mississippi, 1870–1980*. Jackson: University Press of Mississippi, 2005.

Burner, Eric. *And Gently He Shall Lead Them: Robert Parris Moses and Civil Rights in Mississippi*. New York: New York University Press, 1994.

Cagin, Seth and Philip Dray. *We Are Not Afraid: The Story of Goodman, Schwerner, and Chaney and the Civil Rights Campaign for Mississippi*. New York: MacMillan, 1988.

Cohodas, Nadine. *The Band Played Dixie: Race and the Liberal Conscience at Ole Miss*. New York: Free Press, 1997.

Crespino, Joseph. *In Search of Another Country: Mississippi and the Conservative Counterrevolution*. Princeton, NJ: Princeton University Press, 2007.

Crosby, Emilye. *A Little Taste of Freedom: The Black Freedom Struggle in Claiborne County, Mississippi*. Chapel Hill: University of North Carolina Press, 2005.

Curry, Constance. *Silver Rights*. San Diego: Harcourt Brace, 1995.

Danielson, Chris. *After Freedom Summer: How Race Realigned Mississippi Politics, 1965–1986*. Gainesville: University Press of Florida, 2011.

Dittmer, John. *Local People: The Struggle for Civil Rights in Mississippi*. Urbana: University of Illinois Press, 1994.

Doyle, William. *An American Insurrection: James Meredith and the Battle of Oxford, Mississippi, 1962*. New York: Anchor Books, 2003.

Eagles, Charles W. *Civil Rights, Culture Wars: The Fight over a Mississippi Textbook*. Chapel Hill: University of North Carolina Press, 2017.

Eagles, Charles W. *The Price of Defiance: James Meredith and the Integration of Ole Miss*. Chapel Hill: University of North Carolina Press, 2009.

Gallagher, Henry T. *James Meredith and the Ole Miss Riot: A Soldier's Story*. Jackson: University Press of Mississippi, 2012.

Gorn, Elliott. *Let the People See: The Story of Emmett Till*. New York: Oxford University Press, 2018.

Goudsouzian, Aram. *Down to the Crossroads: Civil Rights, Black Power, and the Meredith March Against Fear*. New York: Farrar, Straus, and Giroux, 2014.

Hamlin, Françoise N. *Crossroads at Clarksdale: The Black Freedom Struggle in the Mississippi Delta after World War II*. Chapel Hill: University of North Carolina Press, 2012.

Hendrickson, Paul. *Sons of Mississippi: A Story of Race and Its Legacy*. New York: Vintage, 2003.

Irons, Jenny. *Reconstituting Whiteness: The Mississippi State Sovereignty Commission*. Nashville: Vanderbilt University Press, 2010.

Katagiri, Yasuhiro. *The Mississippi State Sovereignty Commission: Civil Rights and States' Rights*. Jackson: University Press of Mississippi, 2001.

Lambert, Frank. *The Battle of Ole Miss: Civil Rights v. States' Rights*. New York: Oxford University Press, 2010.

Lee, Chana Kai. *For Freedom's Sake: The Life of Fannie Lou Hamer*. Urbana: University of Illinois Press, 1999.

Lord, Walter. *The Past That Would Not Die*. New York: Harper & Row, 1965.

Luckett Jr., Robert E. *Joe T. Patterson and the White South's Dilemma: Evolving Resistance to Black Advancement*. Jackson: University Press of Mississippi, 2015.

Marsh, Charles. *God's Long Summer: Stories of Faith and Civil Rights*. Princeton, NJ: Princeton University Press, 1997.

McAdam, Doug. *Freedom Summer*. New York: Oxford University Press, 1988.

McMillen, Neil R. *The Citizens' Council: Organized Resistance and the Second Reconstruction, 1954–64*. Urbana: University of Illinois Press, 1971.

McMillen, Neil R. *Dark Journey: Black Mississippians in the Age of Jim Crow*. Urbana: University of Illinois Press, 1989.

Meredith, James H. *Three Years in Mississippi*. Jackson: University Press of Mississippi, 2019. Original 1966.

Meredith, James H. and William Doyle. *A Mission from God: A Memoir and Challenge for America*. New York: Atria Books, 2016.

Mills, Kay. *This Little Light of Mine: The Life of Fannie Lou Hamer*. New York: Dutton, 1993.

Mills, Nicolaus. *Like a Holy Crusade: Mississippi 1964—The Turning Point of the Civil Rights Movement in America*. Chicago: Ivan R. Dee, 1992.

Morris, Tiyi M. *Womanpower Unlimited and the Black Freedom Struggle in Mississippi*. Athens: University of Georgia Press, 2015.

Moye, J. Todd. *Let the People Decide: Black Freedom and White Resistance Movements in Sunflower County, Mississippi, 1945–1986*. Chapel Hill: University of North Carolina Press, 2004.

Newman, Mark. *Divine Agitators: The Delta Ministry and Civil Rights in Mississippi*. Athens: University of Georgia Press, 2004.

O'Brien, M. J. *We Shall Not Be Moved: The Jackson Woolworth's Sit-In and the Movement It Inspired*. Jackson: University Press of Mississippi, 2014.

Oshinsky, David M. *Worse than Slavery: Parchman Farm and the Ordeal of Jim Crow Justice*. New York: The Free Press, 1996.

Parker, Frank R. *Black Votes Count: Political Empowerment in Mississippi after 1965*. Chapel Hill: University of North Carolina Press, 1990.

Payne, Charles M. *I've Got the Light of Freedom: The Organizing Tradition and the Mississippi Freedom Struggle*. Berkeley: University of California Press, 1995.

Rogers, Kim Lacy. *Life and Death in the Delta: African American Narratives of Violence, Resilience, and Social Change*. New York: Palgrave Macmillan, 2006.

Silver, James W. *Mississippi: The Closed Society*. New Enlarged Edition. New York: Harcourt, Brace and World, 1966. Original 1963.

Spofford, Tim. *Lynch Street: The May 1970 Slayings at Jackson State College*. Kent, OH: Kent State University Press, 1988.

Tell, Dave. *Remembering Emmett Till*. Chicago: University of Chicago Press, 2019.

Thompson, Julius Eric. *The Black Press in Mississippi, 1865–1985*. Gainesville: University Press of Florida, 1993.

Tyson, Timothy B. *The Blood of Emmett Till*. New York: Simon and Schuster, 2017.

Umoja, Akinyele Omowale. *We Will Shoot Back: Armed Resistance in the Mississippi Freedom Movement*. New York: New York University Press, 2013.

Vollers, Maryann. *Ghosts of Mississippi: The Murder of Medgar Evers, the Trials of Byron De La Beckwith, and the Haunting of the New South*. Boston: Little, Brown and Company, 1995.

Watson, Bruce. *Freedom Summer: The Savage Season That Made Mississippi Burn and Made America a Democracy*. New York: Viking, 2010.

Williams, Michael Vinson. *Medgar Evers: Mississippi Martyr*. Fayetteville: University of Arkansas Press, 2011.

Williamson, Joy Ann. *Radicalizing the Ebony Tower: Black Colleges and the Black Freedom Struggle in Mississippi*. New York: Teachers College Press, 2008.